The Roots of Religious Doubt
and the Search for Security

The Roots of Religious Doubt and the Search for Security

Vernon W. Grant

A CROSSROAD BOOK
The Seabury Press · New York

The Seabury Press
815 Second Avenue
New York, N.Y. 10017

Copyright © 1974 by The Seabury Press, Inc.
Designed by Paula Wiener
Printed in the United States of America

LIBRARY OF CONGRESS CATALOGING IN PUBLICATION DATA

Grant, Vernon W
   The roots of religious doubt and the search for security.

   "A Crossroad book."
   Bibliography: p.
   1. Religion—Philosophy. 2. Belief and doubt.
I. Title.
BL51.G724   248   74-9779
ISBN 0-8164-1165-4

Contents

Introduction, 1

1 Issues of Ultimate Concern, 13

2 Meaning in Evolution, 40

3 Evolution and Ethics, 66

4 Meaning in History, 82

5 Theologies of Nature, 115

6 Psychological Solutions, 147

Appendix Notes, 211

References, 229

The Roots of Religious Doubt
and the Search for Security

Introduction

THIS book has had two main sources: one, the encounters of a clinical psychologist working in psychiatric settings with problems in the borderland between religion and psychology. The other, copious evidence that colleagues were being confronted with similar experiences.

The encounters began as patient-therapist relationships. The central concerns were anxiety, depression and lowered morale linked with the loss or weakening of religious faith. Some of the people were neurotic to a degree. Most were definitely not, and therefore would not be classed as "patients" in the usual sense. In either case the problems were clearly separable from any kind of emotional disorder. In those that offered the clearest and most direct challenge the individuals were nonneurotic, reflective and of above-average intelligence.

In each instance the writer found himself responding in two different ways: one in terms of the individuality of the person seeking help; the other to the more basic problem of the religious issue presented. Among the latter were questions that led far beyond the usual margins of the work of a clinician, and here he was often less a therapist than a fellow inquirer.

Dr. Carl Jung once made a statement which has often been quoted in this context: "Among all my patients . . . over thirty-five . . . there has not been one whose problem in the last resort was not that of finding a religious outlook on life. It is safe to say that every one of them fell ill because he had lost that which the living religions of every age have given to their followers, and none of them has been really healed who did not regain his religious outlook." [7]

The statement is in line with the observation by Anton Boisen that "in mental disorder we are dealing with a problem which is essentially spiritual." Victor Frankl has also written that "continually a psychiatrist is approached today by patients who confront him with human problems rather than neurotic symptoms. Some people who nowadays call on a psychiatrist would have seen a pastor, priest or rabbi in former days . . . so that the doctor is confronted with philosophical questions rather than emotional conflicts." [5]

In his book *The Crisis in Psychiatry and Religion*, Prof. O. H. Mowrer has called attention to "the fact that so many psychologists are now turning their research interests toward problems which have long been of concern to religious and church leaders." In certain areas, he believes it "inevitable that psychologists should encounter many of the same realities as have interested religious thinkers and practitioners throughout history." [9]

The loss or weakening of religious faith may be sudden, when precipitated by a traumatic incident, or gradual and without a specific factor. Its emotional side may be prominent, expressed in depression and anxiety. The emotional reaction may, on the other hand, be relatively subdued, the change being mainly "intellectual," in the form of an altered perception of reality.

A professional man in his forties described the experience as follows:

The turning point in my religious life came with the revelations about Auschwitz, Dachau, Treblinka and the other torture and extermination centers. The shock was gradual over a period of months as the meaning of it penetrated. The main thing was a change in my "picture" of the world. I had always thought that there was a limit to evil, something to do with its meaning. I had believed or felt that it had a role of some kind in life, or that it was a means to some end.

I have not been able to think it all through and I'm still baffled, but one thing is terribly clear. I no longer believe that there is a limit to evil or that human misfortunes always somehow have a larger meaning. I don't believe that a good always comes out of it. In other words I believe in "absolute" evil.

Another way of describing it is to say that what I think of as the reality of things has turned cold and impersonal. *Anything* can happen. I've had spells of real anxiety, not because I'm afraid of any particular misfortune but because it's like living in a different world. The trust is gone. I'm more affected than ever before by the misfortunes of others. The thought that I could be next is very real and frightening. I feel there is nothing to turn to for moral support except the people close to me, people I can be sure are my friends. I'd say that this has become a much more important part of my life.

For a university student the change was similarly gradual, occurring for the most part under the stimulus of academic experiences. Here a well-established religious orientation was progressively undermined.[A] *

---

* The symbol (A) in the text refers to the Appendix notes.

I was raised in a rural area. My family were Baptists. Going to church was a regular part of life. I never realized until recently how completely I took religious premises for granted. I mean that everything was part of a "plan" with rewards and punishments and "accepting Christ" as the real center of life on earth. I'm sure I never doubted that Christ was the son of God and that he was sent to earth to help save man. To me Christ was the absolute proof that there was a God and I never doubted immortality or that this life was just a beginning, a kind of preparation for the real thing.

In my first year at college I took a course in philosophy that really opened my eyes. I don't think the teacher ever actually tried to make us doubt or to question our faith. All he ever said about the purpose of the course was that it was to "make us think about some fundamentals."

What happened was that I learned that almost nothing that I had accepted was true and certain beyond question. There was pro and con on every issue. The greatest thinkers who had ever lived were not agreed on the most basic things. I had been living on what I thought were "absolutes." Well, I discovered that there weren't any such things. It was all a matter of possibility and speculation. I was really astonished to find that some very great men, great thinkers, did not even believe in a life after death.

I guess the best way of putting it is that the foundation is gone, with nothing to put in its place. Life looks very different to me now. In fact you could say it's like living in a different world. There are so few things left to feel sure about. Life has become just living in the here and now, with nothing ahead you could call a real future. It's sort of bleak and lonely. Sometimes I feel lost and afraid. Back home with my folks it's hard to believe I ever thought the way they do. They're upset about me because I'm a lot less happy than I used to be. I'm surely not as happy as they are. At bottom I guess it's a matter of security. Deep down security.

A housewife in her middle thirties sought psychiatric help after a suicide attempt which followed the death of her husband in an automobile accident. A few months earlier her mother had died of influenza. The depression was traceable in part to the short interval between the two losses.

My husband was the finest human being I've ever known. He was honest and generous and thoughtful of others; just an all around good person. Everybody liked him. He was completely blameless in the accident that killed him, yet he died after many hours of terrible pain.

My mother was widowed early in her marriage. She had had to work very hard to carry the burden of raising the family without help. Her death came just when things were getting easier for her, when she was about to have a chance to enjoy life free of worry and pressure and labor.

I became suicidal because I felt so strongly that I did not want to live in a world in which such things could happen. I had tried hard to convince myself that there must be some kind of meaning, even in spite of all the anguish and the shock.

Well, I failed. It was just too cruel and too terribly unfair. It was more than depression or despair that made me "want out." I just hated life. I simply could not accept it. I rejected it. I did not want to be a part of it any longer.

The reference here to "some kind of meaning" implies some degree of belief that certain personal experiencs do and *must* have significance that extends beyond the surface of the event itself. The belief may not be clearly formulated, and may never have come to awareness except in time of crisis. Such implicit premises appear to be common. The wife of one of my patients told me that the only evidence of religious belief or "assumption" she had ever observed in her husband was his comment, at the time of a serious illness, that he had "led an upright life" and so found such a visitation beyond his understanding. The issue raised in the Biblical story of Job—that of seemingly altogether blameless misfortune—is probably one of the most frequent in popular religious thinking at times of crises.

The branch of medicine known as psychosomatics is based, as Gordon Allport has observed, on "recognition of the all important fact that what a man believes profoundly affects his health, both mental and physical." [1] What he believes about many things—his work, his marriage, his future—can be vital in this sense, but what he believes about life's meaning as a whole must rank high in any scale of values. "Religious belief, simply because it deals with fundamentals, often turns out to be the most important belief of all." [8]

One of the marks of a mature person, Dr. Allport suggests, is a life philosophy of some kind. A strong interest or sense of purpose tends to unify behavior, to organize thoughts and feelings and reduce the likelihood of conflicts. An absorbing nonreligious interest, scientific, esthetic or social, may serve well. But all such motivations must finally fail to meet the need for answers to the truly basic questions. "A cause may be absorbing, but it seldom includes the whole of a mature person's horizon. Residues are left over which only religion can absorb." [2]

A writer on the philosophy of religion believes that most men, beyond the ordinary needs for food, shelter, companionship and achievement, "feel a more general and comprehensive need, the need of integrating the scattered and more or less conflicting parts of themselves . . . into a coherent and effective unity. This is the vital good that religious faith in the past has brought to men." [10] It has often been said that man must be regarded as a "naturally religious animal" since no human society has ever been found without beliefs and practices which may be defined as religious. Man "is the being who asks the question of the ground and goal of his life and exhibits . . . need for some answer . . ." Concern with the ultimate purpose is vital because it gives meaning to all other concerns. Since all human cultures exhibit a religious "dimension," it may be regarded as part of the basic structure of existence.

The depressions and anxieties, the lowered or shattered morale that may follow upon religious crises, whether sudden or gradual, are emphatically not to be regarded as evidence of "character weakness." Challenging the meaning of life, as Viktor Frankl says, "can . . . never be taken as a manifestation of morbidity or abnormality; it is rather the truest expression of the state of being human, the mark of the most human nature in man." [6] Man alone of all animals, he observes, is capable of questioning the meaning of his existence.

The people with whom issues of this kind were discussed were consciously exploring outside the area of orthodox religious doctrine. Often such probing into a world view alien to their upbringing was accompanied by anxiety. Fundamental questions were raised in both group and individual therapy sessions. If "God is dead"—meaning the "old" God—what is the new one like, if there is to be a new one? Unless there is a "purpose" at work in the universe, why was it ever begun (did God *need* it)? Why, if God represents supreme wisdom and benevolence, did he make life such an enigma that great thinkers have confessed to being baffled? What have the "scientific" philosophers to offer, if anything, to replace the faith that traditional religion has provided? What can psychology offer to "hold a person up" if he has lost the faith in which he was raised?

Professor Allport noted, in his study *The Individual and His Religion*, that while churchmen have long been inclined toward the inclusion of psychology and psychiatry in their preparation for the ministry there has been no corresponding inclination toward philosophy and theology on the part of the other two professions. It would seem that psychiatrists and psychologists *are as much obligated* to do this as they themselves regard the clergy as in need of study of the behavioral sciences.

The writer decided to accept this obligation, not with the intention of becoming an amateur philosopher-theologian but of reviewing, as thoroughly as possible, fields outside of the orthodox approaches to the issues encountered. This meant, in his case, an effort to discover what could be gleaned from these fields by one who had long been free of any reference frame in terms of traditional religious doctrine. This is mentioned only to indicate that the effort was not biased by any motive to justify, salvage or support an already accepted set of premises. It was not to be a seeking to "make a case," but only to explore for possible grounds for a faith, meaning some degree of *belief*, among the established findings in certain selected areas. Among these are the psychology and philosophy of religion, some interpretations of human history and of the findings of evolutionary biology.

With reference to the "obligation" indicated above, it is obvious that a psychologist who thus ventures beyond the limits of his professional competence is under question to justify such a project. In answer to this I would include: (1) what I feel is a fair degree of intimacy in understanding of the needs of those who may be seeking help of this kind, based upon many direct encounters, some

over a considerable period, in psychiatric or clinical counseling settings; (2) experiences, through many years of
individual and group psychotherapy, during those phases
in which such basic issues arose, pointing to what appeared
to be most essential in meeting those needs. These led also
to some convictions as to the role of certain social factors
in supplying emotional supports of the kind which serve
to replace, at least in part, what traditional religion has
ceased to be able to offer to increasing numbers of people;
and (3) a long-standing personal interest in the fundamental issues involved, dating from early encounters with
philosophical problems (in the course of teaching the history of psychology); from a few years of teaching college
biology and evolutionary theory; finally, a lifelong interest
in and concern with human history with special reference
to interpretation of its meaning and generalizations.

A biologist writing a few years ago on Nature and
God ventured in the preface of his book an answer to
a query he surmised some fellow scientists might make.
Since I feel exactly as he did I can do no better than to
quote him:

> My scientific colleagues might well say, "Cobbler, stick to
> your last." But we have been doing that in science for long
> enough. I have attempted what is not a very popular en-
> deavour in our generation. It is to cover a canvas so broad
> that the whole cannot possibly be the specialized knowledge
> of any single person. The attempt may be presumptuous. I
> have made it because of the urgency that we try, in spite of
> the vastness of the subject. I would not have written had I
> not discovered something for myself that makes sense of the
> world of specialized knowledge in which I live.[4]

While no single theme, interpretation or point of view
of any originality has been set forth, the study does present
an integration of materials which may be classed under

the general heading of naturalistic philosophy. While there are many books of comparable aim and coverage, I know of none which offers a treatment at the level attempted here. I have consistently striven for clarity and concreteness, and so far as the material itself has permitted, for simplicity of expression. It may not be necessary to add that the orientation with which the book concludes is, if not one of optimism, at least that of a "working hypothesis" positive in tone and posture, and that it should offer support, if not an elevation, for the morale of those who may have been to some degree affected by the doubts and questionings touched upon in this section, and especially in that to follow.

In a few of the encounters with the "spiritually troubled" which led to this study, orthodox religious premises were still well established. These people appeared to need, in the main, supportive help or instruction in doctrinal matters. They were referred to churchmen. In most of the cases, however, it was clear that religious moorings of the traditional kind had been abandoned, faith weakened or lost. *These* people were seeking outside of organized religion for answers to some one or more of the fundamental questions. Among the foremost: What *can* one believe or have faith in? It was implicit that *something* to believe was necessary.

One aspect of the orientation to be offered here is therefore what is most commonly called "natural" theology in the broadest sense, meaning interpretations of nature and of the *natural* experiences of mankind. The term has been used for "any theology not based on Biblical revelation." So wide a view forces selection. This part of the study is essentially an integration of materials and themes with a conscious effort to avoid personal bias but with equal awareness that the effort could not possibly be fully successful. I would stress only that in all areas beyond the limits of psychology I have relied exclusively on the findings and views of the best available authorities on the topics included. In this context the posture adopted has been well formulated by Ian Barbour: both scientist and theologian live in the same world and it would surely be a paradox if some of the questions they seek to answer were not common to both. "If the theologian speaks of God's activity in nature, his statements cannot ignore the scientists' discoveries about the character of the natural order. Again, the theologian raises distinctive questions about the character of human existence, but he is referring to the same creature whose relation to nature is under scrutiny by the scientist." [3]

The text proper begins with four documentary studies whose main value lies in the fairly sharp profiles with which they present some of the most fundamental issues and questions of the philosophy of religion. The first illustrates, very briefly, the perennial problem of severe human distress which appears to have no discoverable justifying or constructive features of any kind. It symbolizes what has many times been acknowledged, in one phrasing or another, as the rock on which all traditional religions have foundered: the problem of "evil."

The second, simple in outline, describes the discovery that some kinds of evil are juite certainly *built into* the structure of nature, the issue here clearly bypassing all views of suffering as having its final source in the sinful behavior of mankind.

The next case is given at some length because of the several vital issues covered. Being unusually clear in expression it is given in the words of the person concerned. Here the concept of "divine compensation" is examined, likewise the familiar doctrine, extended to cosmic dimensions, that divine purpose may justify any means.

The final document presents a query less often included

in the literature of this sphere of discussion, but nonetheless relevant: the seeming lack of personal development or fulfillment in what is probably an impressively large number of human lives. In place of the idea of life's absurdity, as stressed by certain "existential" writers, the issue appears to be rather that of its pointlessness. Evolution, as the biologist views it, being the outstanding phenomenon of life on earth, its seeming failure in the individual instance looks like a valid item for the roster of fundamental questions.

CHAPTER 1

Issues of Ultimate Concern

T H E case studies to be presented are those of persons who reacted with depression or anxiety to experiences which raised deeply disturbing and basic questions. None of these persons had been affected to a degree suggesting an excessive reaction. There were no histories of emotional disorder. None, in brief, could be classed as neurotic. This is stressed in order to indicate the episodes as all within the range of normal human emotional stress.

The central questions are summarized in introductory statements of the queries presented

CASE NO. 1

Question: *How is the kind of human suffering which cannot be interpreted as a learning, growth, or corrective experience to be reconciled with the concept of life as purposive?*

This rather simple case presents features doubtless familiar to every pastoral counselor. A thirty-six-year-old man had lost his nine-year-old daughter, who succumbed to leukemia after many weeks of suffering, much of it acute. He had become too depressed to work, had taken a month's leave of absence, which he spent traveling about the country with his wife. Time had healed his grief to some degree, but had not stilled some questions raised by the shock of his loss. He felt he could understand physical or mental pain as a learning experience or as a means of enriching the understanding and the sympathies, but he was unable to interpret the agonies of his child in this way. The fact that the child had been obedient and responsive, conscientious and altogether lovable, made it harder for him to find such a meaning in her death.

He could not accept the view suggested by his pastor that the child's death was in some way a means to the end that his own and his family's spiritual development would be somehow forwarded by the loss. Sacrifice of any human being for some larger design was to him only an application of the corrupting doctrine that a sufficient goal can justify any means used to achieve it. No larger purpose of any kind, he felt, could qualify or relieve the basic brutality that takes an individual life in this way, such a philosophy being "communistic" and inherently un-christian.

CASE NO. 2

Question: *How is the victimizing of the weak by the strong, seen throughout the animal world, to be reconciled with the concept of a just and benevolent deity?*

A business executive in his early fifties had had a heart

attack requiring several weeks of bed rest, during which his reading included some natural history. Though an educated man with considerable background in science, he became aware for the first time that, as he put it, "the entire organization of animal nature is based on exploitation. I mean the hierarchy in which each species lives on a 'lower' one and is in turn victimized by one 'above.' A frog devours insects and is itself devoured by a pelican, and so on." The old phrase "Nature red in tooth and claw" acquired a much larger meaning; the beak and talons of the hawk, the poison fangs of the snake, became symbols of life as a deadly and perpetual competition.

It was in applying this symbol at the human level that the major reorientation in his thinking occurred. The predatory behavior of aggressor nations and the long record of wars of conquest he had seen as evils, but only as expressions of man's willful perversity or of his failure to apply a code of morality to the behavior of whole societies. Such aggression he had assumed was "wrong in the sight of God" as well as to all men of goodwill. What he now saw was that this assumption was false. Not only was exploitation of the essence of the subhuman world; man, like all animals, is a born predator. "It is no greater crime for one man to kill another than for one animal to kill another; or rather, both are crimes. But both are equally *natural*, and therefore, if there is a responsible deity, both are divinely sanctioned."

He found that he could not reconcile what he called his "new biology" with the doctrines of his religion. He was troubled enough to solicit an interview with a clergyman, but was left unsatisfied with the answer that faith must suffice where understanding fails, and that trust must be placed in God as a child trusts a parent in matters too abstruse for comprehension. My client's comment was that faith such as this could be the answer only as a name for belief founded solely on a need to escape the facts (recalling a familiar definition of the term as "believing what you know is not true").

CASE NO. 3

This subject finds inherent absurdity in the concept of "compensation"—as by way of an afterlife—for injustices which are part of the basic structure of existence. Question: *How can such injustices be reconciled with faith in a benevolent and omnipotent creator? How are we to interpret the phenomenon of the human predator, in view of his direct lineage with the predatory lower animals?*

A forty-three-year-old physician sought counseling partly at the request of his wife, and partly out of curiosity as to the reaction of a clinical psychologist to his problem of depression and anxiety. He did not regard his problem as psychiatric. He brought with him a copy of a letter he had written to a close friend who had learned of his depression and become concerned about him. The main body of this letter follows:

I think what really started all this was something quite trivial on the surface. It was a conversation with a friend whose nine-year-old son is a bit retarded and has a speech impediment. His behavior has marked him so that he is constantly being jeered at and made the butt of jokes by other children. He often comes home from school crying. Of course his father feels awful about it.

I began to think about this in a way I never had before. I mean about unfortunate people with defects. This boy will be handicapped all his life. I began to ask questions of myself. If there is an ultimate meaning,—an *ethic*—in our existence, there has got to be some kind of justification for this. I guess I have always had this idea about any sort of misfortune having nothing to do with personal behavior.

Then for the first time in my life, it struck me that this kind of logic is ridiculous. I mean the idea of compensation, as in an after-life, as if the Creator of a Universe would be making amends for the blunders or failures in his handiwork. I say failures because it's awfully hard for me to think of that little kid's blameless suffering as the *intention* of a just Deity. And I say blunders because I once saw a medical book with pictures of infants born with all kinds of deformities, like misshapen heads, or an arm sticking out of the chest, or no rectum. If God had the power to "compensate," why wouldn't he have prevented such disasters at outset?

Then one night I saw a documentary film that showed a lion bringing down a deer, jumping on its back and breaking the neck with its teeth. Then the thought hit me, *this* is no defect in the design, like a deformed child; this is *part* of the design. What happened to that deer is inherent in the structure of nature. Maybe you will think I was pretty naive, but I felt like I was waking up from a trance. I had never before thought of carnivorous animals in this way. It was like looking at a familiar word and suddenly reading a new meaning in it.

Every kind of human predator, the great conquerors—Alexander, Caesar, Genghis Khan and Tamerlane, the Huns and Mongols—are all naturals: preying is as basic in the human as in the animal world. The individual we call a criminal, in every age of history, is a *natural* in the same sense. And if criminal action is an evil, then evil is inherent in the very structure of man's being.

All this time I had been fighting for something to hang onto that would give support for faith, but this was the turning point, and the turn was downward. I kept coming back to little Herbie (the retarded boy) too, and the fact that he was no "mistake." All the inequalities of mankind are just as basic as the differences in size and strength that enable one animal to prey on another. And all the cruelties the superior man has inflicted on the inferior throughout the whole of history are equally inherent in the structure. Men prey on each other as well as on the lower animals, and in their turn are victimized by the pathogenic bacteria.

This new perception is still very strange, and at times hard to grasp. H. G. Wells wrote, just before he died, that a "frightful queerness" had come into life. That is exactly how I felt. But Wells was wrong. The "queerness" was always there. He was apparently seeing it for the first time. It comes with the realization that there may be no "justification," that the universe is amoral.

This all sounds harsh and brutal, and I am not forgetting that there is love in the world too; love of the altruistic kind. But the fact of love does not offset the terribly cruel basic pattern. That was there for an infinity of time before love "began," and it is *still* active throughout the whole of nature.

CASE NO. 4

Question: *If the purpose of our existence is assumed to be the development of some kind and degree of insight, "wisdom," or "spiritual growth," why, in so many human lives, is there little or no evidence of these processes?*

A woman of forty-two, consulting a counselor regarding problems of adjusting to her sixty-five-year-old mother, who had recently come to live with her, spoke as follows:

I remember my mother clearly as she was when I was a child and I do not recall that she was ever any different from the way she is now. She was never affectionate, always hard to please, rarely praised me or anyone else but often criticized. She never acknowledged a fault or a mistake, but frequently blamed others. She often talked about the neighbors, nearly always critically and unfavorably. She and my father seemed to tolerate each other rather than need and love each other. She was religious in a narrow kind of way, more concerned with personal salvation than with practicing Christian virtues.

My father and I used to say: perhaps she will mellow and soften when she gets older, but she never did. If anything the traits I've described became more noticeable.

In certain moods, thinking about her, I've wondered what life is really for. I suppose there are lots of people like her. I mean with different personalities but not changing much. I can't see that she has made any kind of progress as a person. She has rarely seemed happy, more as if she were just enduring things. It seems to me that she has been at a standstill most of her life. Such a narrow, limited sort of existence.

Philosophic discussions of "purposiveness" in organic evolution and in human history usually entail broad surveys and often abstract speculations, but the character of individual personality change with the passage of time seems to come close to the heart of the matter. One of the vital and concrete testing grounds for views about "purposiveness" must be the individual life history.[A]

Development of the Issues

How seriously are the questions raised in these examples to be taken? The persons who raised them were laymen, not philosophers or "deep thinkers." It is reasonable to query at the outset as to the status of these issues among those in a position to judge them—the professional students of such fundamental problems.

It may be said with assurance that all these issues have been acknowledged with respect in the literature of the related fields of philosophy and religion, where their contents have little novelty. Our illustrative cases are mainly of value as clear expressions of the conflicts and perplexities likely to be encountered by people involved in experiences which concern the basic meanings of existence and the security of religious faith.

The first, despite its apparent simplicity, introduces what is seemingly so natural a part of life itself as to be as much taken for granted as the air we breathe: the elemental fact of apparently blameless human distress. Plagues, floods, droughts and famines, earthquakes and hurricanes, have been, somewhere in the world, an almost continuous part of human experience throughout its known course. All are aspects of the "problem of evil," and under this label the subject of a fair-sized library of discussion, doctrine and speculation. Considering it in its largest dimension, a writer on the philosophy of history states: "The outstanding element . . . out of which an interpretation of history could arise . . . is the basic experience of evil and suffering. . . . The interpretation of history is, in the last analysis, an attempt to understand . . . the meaning of suffering. . . ." Another writes that no philosophy can overlook "the generally wretched lot of the great masses of men in all previous societies, and the general acceptance of wretchedness as the law of nature of the will of God." [16]

A distinction is needed at the outset between two varieties of human distress, since one has been much the more difficult to interpret. The first concerns experiences of any kind which have value as a means of learning or of personal growth. It is a rudiment of psychology that much of the growth of personality is stimulated by challenges of some kind. We become stronger, more resourceful, through frustrations and defeats, or emergencies that demand mobilization of effort. Without them we remain at a standstill and only mark time.

Whatever suffering occurs in stress situations may be seen as justified by its outcome as in some way creative. The distress, along with the effort, is compensated. There is a reward; therefore life is fair, and what appears at first as sheer misfortune is seen to have meaning. In the background of this philosophy is, of course, the premise that one of the purposes of our existence is a learning experience of some kind. A housewife whose marriage was blighted by neurotic jealousy was able, after recovery, to find compensations. "I see now, not only how my insecurity caused me to misinterpret my husband's behavior, but how it affected my relationships with others as well. I understand better how to relate to others, and that marriage is is first of all a human relationship, like any other. It has been a painful ordeal, but it should save a lot of grief in the future, so I guess you could say it has been worthwhile, or will be, in the end."

The unanswered question, and the essential source of much of the problem of evil, arises only when such a view is impossible, not because a growth opportunity is unrecognized but because it is absent. The suffering may teach no lesson, have no outcome. The trauma may result in no moral advance or insight. Challenges can be too great for the resources; defeats bring no gain of any kind. The experience may shatter completely; the outcome may be psychosis, demoralization or death.

The climactic case, which has perhaps become the outstanding symbol of the "kingdom of evils," is that seen in the context of tragedy in childhood. Here, the issue is at its sharpest because innocence is most concretely apparent. Also, doubtless, because the emotional response here awakens vibrations in the parental chord in all or most of us.

It is vividly expressed in some passages of Dostoevsky

which tell of the torture and death of the child of a peasant in punishment for an accidental and blameless offense against a Russian aristocrat. Out of this the novelist makes an indictment against *any* suffering which is innocent because incurred unknowingly, or which is followed by death, or for which no "justification" is conceivable. The basic and "cosmic" question is raised: How are such events to be understood as somehow purposeful as means to *mankind's* ultimate goal or happiness (here called "eternal harmony")?

For the hundredth time, I repeat, there are numbers of questions, but I've only taken the children because in their case what I mean is so unanswerably clear. Listen! If all must suffer to pay for the eternal harmony, what have children to do with it? . . . It's beyond all comprehension why they should suffer, and why they should pay for the harmony. . . . And if it is really true that they must share responsibility for all their fathers' crimes, such a truth is not of this world and is beyond my comprehension . . . so I renounce the higher harmony altogether. It's not worth the tears of that one tortured child. . . . It's not worth it, because those tears are unatoned for. They must be atoned for, or there can be no harmony. . . . And if the sufferings of children go to swell the sum of sufferings which was necessary to pay for truth, then I protest that the truth is not worth such a price. . . . I don't want harmony. From love of humanity I don't want it. . . . I would rather remain in my unavenged suffering and unsatisfied indignation . . .⁵

Suffering that is without beneficent outcome of any discernible kind has been the center of the problem of evil for centuries. When accepted as a factual reality, the ancient query as to its meaning was stated in perhaps its simplest form by David Hume: "Is Deity willing to prevent evil, but not able: Then he is impotent. Is he able but not willing: Then he is malevolent. Is he both able and willing? Whence then is evil?" [9]

The key word above is of course "discernible." Here patently is the core of the issue: that it is too much to expect of the finite mind that it should grasp the designs of the Infinite. Some would doubtless add that it is high presumption for the finite mind to question or reject this kind of evil on the ground that its role in the design is not apparent.

A traditional answer is illustrated with a concrete image by a professor of philosophy. "The appearance of evil is due to our limited and partial vision. A discord in a musical composition might be unpleasant if sounded alone. But when we hear it as a part of the whole piece we see that it contributes to the beauty of the whole. In the same way evil would cease to appear as evil if we could view the universe in a single all-embracing vision.* [27]

While such a view, in effect, denies the "true" reality of evil, it also evades the basic issue. If man's limited vision is responsible for so enormous and convincing an experience as evil, then the limitation must itself be regarded as no less a wrong. The problem exists however—as is usually stressed—only if we take for granted at outset

---

* The history of this rationale for evil is a long one. Thus an ancient philosopher (Plotinus) writes: "We are like men who, knowing little of painting, blame the artist because the colors in his picture are not all beautiful—not seeing that he has given to each part what was appropriate to it." Everything in the world is good, he tells us, but goodness is present in a vast number of degrees, and what we call evil are only the lowest degrees of goodness. There could be no variety in the creation were there not such degrees; perfection is meaningless without imperfections.

As for sufferings of guiltless animals, this is necessary "for the good of the whole." "It is better that one animal should be eaten by another than that it should never have existed at all." [15]

that a morality is inherent in the Great Design. It is commonly assumed that the difference between good and bad applies to the order and purpose of the world. To think of it otherwise, as morally indifferent, is an idea quite foreign to the faiths of our culture. If, on the other hand, we can conceive of good and bad as real only as human experiences rather than as part of an "ethical" universe, then evil no longer exists in the sense implied in Hume's statement. In the philosophy of "scientific naturalism," for example, the problem of evil vanished long ago. "It is . . . simply out of date. Such a question as why there is evil in the world can only be asked by a medieval mind. There is, in reality, no such question for the modern naturalistically minded man." * [28]

Men have understandably tended to think of God as a vastly expanded image of the human mind. The design of a creation of which "purpose," "justice," "good" and "evil" are assumed to be elements is clearly the work of a God who thinks and judges as do human beings. To raise question whether God is "able" or "willing" to do anything about evil is obviously to project human thoughts about ability or intention upon Him.

We may say, then, that the *problem* of evil exists only if we think of deity and the universe in this way. For those who dismiss such projections as too naive to be taken seriously there can be no problem. Those, on the other hand, who have always believed in a deity whose ways are so far from being our ways as to be fully and simply

* An historian writes: "Granted the appearances of cosmic order, with its suggestion of a creative intelligence, one may doubt that it is informed with a moral purpose. In the natural world outside of man, with its ceaseless struggle for survival, there is no evidence whatever of 'a power not ourselves making for righteousness'; and in the history of man the principle of righteousness seems to have emerged very gradually from his own painful efforts, uncertain and unblessed." [20]

accepted as beyond comprehension can also escape it. There will be others, however, for whom neither solution is available, who may be troubled, and perhaps deeply troubled. It is for these that the central aims and themes of this book are intended.

Another facet of the same problem is seen in the second of our illustrative cases. Here the faith of a thoughtful person was shaken when a new meaning of certain familiar facts about the animal world suddenly "dawned" upon him: that the beast of prey is part of the built-in structure of nature. From this it followed that the *human* predator is or may be an equally natural phenomenon. It followed also that wars of conquest, always regarded as a most flagrant evil, are in the direct lineage of the animal predator. Were all animals vegetarian our philosophy of nature could at this point be quite different. For the religious thinker, at least, the carnivore becomes a symbol which raises a highly visible question mark.*

Here we are faced not with accident, disease or malformation which can be read as a defect in an otherwise admirable design. This is clearly an "intentional" part of the normal architecture of nature. With the lower animals we bypass the ethical issues which so often enter discussions of suffering ("evil") at the human level. The carnivore's impulses are as innate as his teeth and claws, his beak and talons. Here the problem strikes rock bottom as a challenge and is part of the background of such state-

---

* A student of early man writes: "If there was ever a loss of innocence in man's past, a feeling of original sin or guilt about killing and eating creatures that had once been his equals or superiors, it would have dated back to the transition times when early hominids were developing their taste for meat." He cites a novel of prehistoric life which refers to "the guilt which primitive man felt as he tore into a doe, and of 'the rich smell of meat and wickedness.' " * (Pfeiffer, J. E. *The Emergence of Man*. New York: Harper & Row, Publishers, Incorporated, 1969, p. 106.)

ments as that of the philosopher of science who writes: "The existence of evil and the tragic element in all life must be taken with utmost seriousness. It constitutes a problem for any doctrine of divine omnipotence, and equally of any natural teleology which is too glib in claiming detailed design in nature." It may also have been among the thoughts of a student of religion who has suggested that those whose faith rests in part upon the "facts of nature" must have led sheltered lives.[14]

The human beast of prey, unlike most others, preys upon his fellows as well as upon many other species. One kind of human preying, commonly called conquest, has been a main factor in the formation of all or most communities larger than the family and the clan. "The state as distinct from tribal organization," writes a sociologist, "begins with the conquest of one race by another." [31] In support of the thesis that force is the origin of the state, an historian cites evidence for the thesis that every state begins with compulsion. "The hunter and the herder, accustomed to danger and skilled in killing, look upon war as but another form of the chase and hardly more perilous; when the woods cease to give them abundant game, or flocks decrease through a thinning pasture, they look with envy upon the ripe fields of the village, they invent with modern ease some plausible reason for attack, they invade, conquer, enslave and rule." [3]

Another statement is more dramatic and closer to the tone of our theme: "A herd of blonde beasts of prey, a race of conquerors and masters, which with all its warlike organization and all its organizing power pounces with its terrible claws upon a population, in numbers possibly tremendously superior, but yet formless . . . such is the origin of the state." [21] In over 3,400 years of recorded history, "only 268 have seen no war." [4]

At the level of the lower carnivores predatory behavior is considered as either outside the sphere of morality or as what an evolutionist has called the "old morality," antedating man with his assumed freedom of choice. Old as it is, however—and it is still fully in force throughout nature—it does have its morality, or code, well expressed in the words of a professional soldier of the last century, and which is still not at all "dated."

Live and let live is no device for an army. . . . Far better is it . . . to be too savage, too cruel, too barbarous, than to possess too much sentimentality and human reasonableness. If the soldier is to be good for anything as a soldier, he must be exactly the opposite of a reasoning and thinking man. . . . War, and even peace, require of the soldier absolutely peculiar standards of morality. The recruit brings with him common moral notions, of which he must seek immediately to get rid. . . . The most barbaric tendencies in men come to life again in war, and for war's uses they are incommensurably good.[11]

The nation as a predator differs little in essentials from those who steal, kill or exploit. An historian cites an ancient view "that there is no difference between the conqueror and the robber except the scale of their operation," that banditry is nothing but the predatory state or nation in miniature. It is illustrated in the reported comment of a pirate to Alexander the Great: "Because I do it with a little ship I am called a robber, and you, because you do it with a great fleet, are called an emperor." [1] The great conquerors of history, writes the subject of our third case: "Alexander, Caesar, Genghis Khan and Tamerlane, the Huns and Mongols, are all *naturals*; preying is as basic in the human as in the animal world."

On a smaller scale but in vastly greater numbers, in all ages, and in almost every society, is the individual predator

—the "criminal" who may also be classed as a "natural" in either or both of two senses. As a product and member of an antisocial group (subculture) he develops a code, mores and loyalties which make his behavior normal for the social world in which he lives.

A "philosophy of evil," must come to terms in some way with the phenomenon of the predatory animal. If the human variety is to be seen—as in the current mode—as mainly a social product, the biological origins of the trends that produced him must be explored. His prototype is clearly visible among his subhuman ancestors.*

The subject of our third case, in contemplating features of the natural order which had undermined his faith, includes among them the basic inequalities among men and the "enormous differences in the quality of lives" which result. Such differences are the origin of some of the major themes of human history. The laws of biology,

---

* An apologist for the traditional image of deity, confronted with the spectacle of cruelty and suffering in the animal world, concedes that there does appear to be "Hell itself visibly in operation around us." He concludes that either the appearance of divine cruelty must be false—that such suffering is *somehow* not really evil—or that an evil entity ("some mighty created power . . . at work for ill") changed the herbivorous animals into flesh eaters and thus "corrupted the animal creation before man appeared." * (Lewis, C. S. *God in the Dock: Essays in Theology and Ethics.* Grand Rapids, Mich.: William B. Eerdmans Publishing Company, 1970, pp. 168, 171.)

In our judgment of evil, he suggests, we are reacting *with* God against a power "whom the Great God does curse, and . . . curses through us . . ." He leaves unanswered the question why a God he believes to be benevolent should have created a power which He then Himself condemns.

The victim of the predatory animal continues to symbolize what has perhaps been the single most refractory aspect of the problem of evil excepting for those who have been able to apply the concept of evolution to deity itself.

writes an historian, "are the fundamental lessons of history." [5] The first law is that life is competitive; the second is that the competition is unequal. In the struggle "for food or mates or power some organisms succeed and some fail." As with other departments of biology, "history remains at bottom a natural selection of the fittest individuals and groups in a struggle wherein goodness receives no favors, misfortunes abound, and the final test is the ability to survive." [6]

The inequalities are inherent; variation is as natural as life itself, increasing with its complexity. "There is very little difference between two healthy jelly-fish; a little more, but still not much, between two monkeys, but the difference between two normal men may easily exceed the difference between a jelly-fish and a monkey." [10] Variations represent, of course, the basis of the origin of new species. Along with varying environments they make the essential method of creative evolution.

This is all well and good, our subject (Case No. 3) would say, but "good" only for the species and for the superior organism. What is to console the vast numbers of nature's underdogs, the "runts of the litter," the individuals, animal or human, who are smaller, weaker, less courageous, less attractive sexually, less intelligent than their fellows? In the concourse of evolution they are expendable. The point to be made is that they are penalized, without fault or choice, for their deficits. Their claims cannot be revoked. They are another of the negative elements in the Grand Design, too basic to be overlooked.

While the nation may be shown by the historical record to be the greatest of the predators, a close second are the competitions between classes within the nation, the upper- and underdogs, the superiors and inferiors. A very large part of human history, it has often been said, has been written in terms of such conflict. At all levels—nation, class and individual—the predator poses a central issue for all discussions of the "immoral order" as a natural phenomenon.*

Dostoevsky's strongly felt rebellion against the suffering of a child symbolizes an issue of much larger dimension: that of all arguments which seek to "explain" the distresses of the present by compensations in the future. As our subject (Case No. 3) puts it: "That man may some day make a Utopia for himself on this earth does not vindicate the cost of all that went before, any more than a well fed lion vindicates the death of a deer."

His quotation concerning "the generally wretched lot of the great masses of men in all previous societies" could be supported by many such observations. A professional historian regards the basic experience of evil and suffering as the truly central problem of human history, whose core meaning, "in the last analysis," lies in the interpretation of human distress.[16] The rejection, in philosophies of history, of the concept of sacrifice of any human life, interests or felicities as *means* to the achievement or forwarding of remote ends is frequently expressed in this context. "The historical greatness of a nation does not make up for the annihilation of one single individual." [17]

---

* "Nature smiles at the union of freedom and equality in our utopias. For freedom and equality are sworn and everlasting enemies, and when one prevails the other dies. Leave men free, and their natural inequalities will multiply. . . . Even when repressed, inequality grows . . . and in the end superior ability has its way. Utopias of equality are biologically doomed . . ." [7]

A biologist, on the basis of observation of over fifty species of birds, "is convinced that despotism is one of the major biological principles; that whenever two birds are together invariably one is despot and the other subservient and both know it." [24] An observer is quoted: "Despotism is the basic idea of the world, indissolubly bound up with all life and existence. On it rests the meaning of the struggle for existence."

Here the idea of compensation—that the future, natural or supernatural, will in some way justify the past, both for the human race and for the individual life—is at issue. The subject of our third case cannot accept it, nor could Dostoevsky, nor can Professor Muller, who insists that "an ultimate harmony does not cancel the immense cost in suffering." Any defense for the sacrifice of one generation for another, as of one individual for another, must go beyond finite ethics and rest upon an act of faith.

The question raised by the lack of *oriented* growth in the individual life course, as illustrated in Case No. 4, differs in centering on the issue of apparent purposelessness rather than of injustice. That all who live must mature in some sense or degree is not in question, but rather that the ceiling of development appears so often very low. Here the thesis is that marked personal growth in such matters as understanding of self and others, in goodwill and charity, in grasp of the realities or of the "art of living," can hardly be regarded as part of the normal course of many or even of most human lives.

What, then, are we here for; or why, if purposive development in *some* direction can be assumed to be built into life, is it so often hard to find any impressive degree of deepening and expansion in the personality?

Anthropologists tell us that, unlike the historic "civilized" societies, in many of those commonly known as primitives change may be relatively small—though never absent—over indefinitely long periods of time. Entire peoples, it seems—like many individuals—may seem almost at a standstill in the living patterns (cultures) which, for the human group, are the equivalent of personality in the individual.

The dimensions of the phenomenon become far larger when the animal world as a whole is included. A biologist has labeled as "immortals" certain creatures which have persisted unchanged for what by human standards is a near-infinity of time.[25] The fact that they are simple in form does not alter the import: life here is fixed apparently for all time; evolution has ceased. An oyster of 200 million years ago "would look perfectly familiar if served in a restaurant today." A familiar-looking lizard (*Sphenodon*) has been almost unchanged in some 150 million years. Fossil forms of insects much as we know them today have been found in rocks 200 million years old, a remarkable fact when the short life-span of the organism is considered, and thus the number of generations represented. "Not only have insects apparently undergone little structural change in many millions of years, but also their habits, at least in many cases, remain the same. This is indicated by many similarities . . . in form and type, to closely related groups today. The ants were divided into castes then as now . . ."[19]

Julian Huxley has observed that every successful animal type exhibits trends toward improvement in the course of its evolution, yet "in the great majority of cases, these trends eventually become stabilized . . . they come to an end, and the type (if it does not die out) continues indefinitely on the same level of organization or specialization; it has exhausted its inherent possibilities of major improvement." * [10]

To assume that absence of development raises a question

---

* Parallels have been seen in the "staggering conservatism" of early man, illustrated for example, in his unchanging tools. "Neanderthal man was using notched and toothed tools nearly two million years after their first appearance in Olduvai deposits." More broadly, "life and myths . . . remained much the same for thousands upon thousands of years, innovation . . . resisted as a matter of sheer instinct." * (Pfeiffer, J. E. *The Emergence of Man*. New York: Harper & Row, Publishers, Incorporated, 1969, pp. 126, 127.)

is itself a relatively new attitude, the idea of "progress" having been for long ages foreign to human thinking about purposes and destinies. A static universe is far older than the dynamic one of modern times. The fact remains that progressive change does occur in individual lives, but that this is true to a far greater degree for some than for others.

From this it may be concluded: (1) that the failure need not signify a meaningless life, since knowledge of divine purpose would reveal that every life is meaningful, however lacking in appearance; (2) that the problem itself is unreal in that it arises only when the human idea of purposiveness is read into the cosmic order. It presumes that God must think in the same way we think; that the infinite logic must be like that of the finite mind; and (3) that the failures are real; that the universe contains failures as well as successes; that life is a trial-and-error process and that living at a standstill is but one of a variety of real imperfections in the Creation.

In the context of religious crises the illustrative cases reviewed are in no way unusual and were selected for clarity of statement and for coverage of the character and variety of the issues presented. The literature of biography and autobiography provides many such examples, some relatively mild in emotional impact, some stressful and dramatic.

Among the better known is an episode through which Leo Tolstoy passed in approaching his fiftieth year.[32]

The novelist, as so many others, had never doubted the basic premises of existence—"had never questioned the universe as to its significance." He had seen many men killed in war, yet "had never questioned the right and wrong of the matter." For many years he had taken the lowly status of the peasants on his estate as a normal part of social reality; then he suddenly began to question his right to ignore it. "Poverty, wretchedness, oppression, soldiering, prisons, Siberia, . . . [were] . . . to him facts as natural as that snow should fall in winter and that rivers should flow seaward."

Whatever the underlying sources, the "awakening" was profound and shaking. For the first time in his life he becomes aware of the stark mysteries of existence, and especially of its evils. He can no longer view it with the detached eye of the literary artist. "He can no longer look upon existence as a mere spectacle, but must persistently inquire as to the meaning . . . the rights and wrongs . . . of everything that happens. . . . His world has broken up . . . paralyzed with terror, he stares into the unmeaning gloom." *

The psychologist William James, writing of "the religion of healthy-mindedness," has called attention to a different breed of the human species. These are men who live, and

---

* In his autobiography Tolstoy describes his prolonged quest for a meaningful foundation for his personal existence, beginning with the fundamental question:

Is there in life any purpose which the inevitable death which awaits me does not undo and destroy? These questions are the simplest in the world. . . . Without an answer to them, it is impossible, as I experienced, for life to go on. "But perhaps," I often said to myself, "there may be something I have failed to notice or to comprehend. It is not possible that this condition of despair should be natural to mankind." And I sought for an explanation in all the branches of knowledge acquired by men. I questioned painfully and protractedly and with no idle curiosity. I sought . . . laboriously and obstinately for days and nights together. I sought like a man who is lost and seeks to save himself—and I found nothing. I became convinced, moreover, that all those who before me had sought for an answer in the sciences have also found nothing. And not only this, but that they have recognized that the very thing which was leading me to despair—the meaningless absurdity of life—is the only incontestable knowledge accessible to man.[30]

have always lived, untouched by the threats and spectacles to which Dostoyevsky and Tolstoy responded so profoundly and painfully. Either through basic temperament, unshakable faith or the ability to steadily block out of thought the possible meanings of the world's suffering, they pass by the "kingdom of evils" with consistent serenity. For these people happiness is congenital. They refuse to think ill of life, and the refusal is final. Like the disciples and followers of St. Francis, "from the outset their religion is one of union with the divine."

As a supreme example of this refusal or inability to acknowledge evil, James cites, as have others, our own Walt Whitman, who confronted with unqualified acceptance and pleasure every aspect of nature and of humankind, who apparently never felt "fretfulness, antipathy, complaint or remonstrance," who never spoke in depreciation "of any nationality or class of men, or time in the world's history . . . not even against any animals, insects, or inanimate things, nor any of the laws of nature, nor any of the results of those laws, such as illness, deformity, and death." He could convey himself in a way that "ends by persuading the reader that men and women, life and death, and all things are divinely good." [12]

Spiritual kinsman to Whitman was Goethe, another apostle of "healthy mindedness." Of the latter's reading of the realities, as they appeared to him, a biographer writes: "The great problem of evil, which men have tormented themselves with since the world began, lost all its terrors in the radiant confidence of his optimism. . . . For Goethe there is no evil; there can be no evil, for God's world is good. What we with our limited understanding call evil is but a darker thread in the weft of life; something that is only the good in disguise that we are unable to penetrate. Evil is the servant of the good, as Mephistopheles is the servant of God." [22]

Goethe's conviction of the ultimate rightness of all things created led naturally and logically to a fatalistic posture. "He accepted life, as he counsels us to accept life, as it comes; not to revolt against it, or to rebel. He saw how some men were born to dark unhappy fates; others to success and glory. To the former his advice is to bear with fortitude, without complaint or regret, the life-burden put upon their shoulders. . . ." [23]

That men of such stature as these could read the data of experience in ways so widely different is an impressive commentary on the variables of human psychology. The fact that Tolstoy worked his way up out of despair, and that Goethe's optimism was seemingly rooted in part in willful blindness to the realities does not alter the fact that two such men could, at any phase of their lives, vary so sharply in total response to the not so greatly unlike worlds in which they lived.

It is notable, too, how much the descriptions of Goethe's buoyant perception of beneficence everywhere he looked resemble the accounts that richly document the literature of religious conversion, this with reference to experiences *after* the achievement of recovery of faith. A sample is provided in a testimonial of Jonathan Edwards:

After this my sense of divine things gradually increased and became more and more lively. . . . The appearance of everything was altered; there seemed to be, as it were, a calm, sweet cast, or appearance of divine glory, in almost everything. God's excellency, his wisdom, his purity and love, seemed to appear in everything. . . . And scarce anything, among all the works of nature, was so sweet to me as thunder and lightning; formerly nothing had been so terrible to me. [8]

James observed that the transformation of the perceived world into a panorama of brighter colors and of fresh and promising meanings is almost the exact opposite of the change into "dreadful unreality and strangeness" sometimes experienced by deeply depressed persons.

The emotional states illustrated in our cases, as earlier indicated, were not depressed in any sense suggestive of underlying instability. The moods might be described, however, as in some respects the opposite of what occurs in religious conversion. Instead of the "new world" of the convert there came "that other sort of newness" in which a world hitherto viewed as at core beneficent and purposive is transformed into a highly uncertain if not sinister phenomenon, charged with threats and ambiguities and above all no longer having an assured meaning.

It is here that these experiences of individuals become linked with important trends in the mentality of our time. A professor of philosophy writes: "The picture of a meaningless world, and a meaningless human life, is . . . the basic theme of much modern art and literature. Certainly it is the basic theme of modern philosophy." We are told that we must, finally, and as soon as we can endure it, "face the truth that there is, in the universe outside of man, no spirituality, no regard for values, no friend in the sky, no help or comfort of any sort." [29]

After an analysis of the problem of evil in relation to the image of a loving God, another student of religion concedes, after rejecting traditional interpretations, that he finds nothing to offer in their place; nothing "that would explain in any rational or ethical way why men suffer as they do. . . . Such suffering remains unjust and inexplicable, haphazard and cruelly excessive. . . . It challenges Christian faith with its utterly baffling, alien, destructive meaninglessness." [8]

If such expressions of doubt have many roots, there are those who believe that the main source is the question that sense can be made of existence itself. "The ultimate insecurity," writes Professor Barbour, "is the threat that life might be meaningless. Modern man often experiences emptiness and purposelessness, sometimes anxiety and futility, and occasionally despair." He quotes W. H. Auden: "We are afraid of pain, but more afraid of silence; for no nightmare of hostile objects could be as terrible as this void."

Our failure to find answers to such basic questions is regarded by some as the core of the modern mood, even though few may have formulated or acknowledged it. "Social critics, philosophers, sociologists, and psychotherapists are raising the cry that alienation and the problems of existence form the sickness of our times." The evidence is now convincing "that people seeking psychotherapy do so in ever increasing numbers because they are deeply dissatisfied with the nature and basis of their living . . . even those who do not seek psychotherapy often feel alone and empty." [18] A student of the "existential neurosis" finds that its nucleus is "meaninglessness, or chronic inability to believe in the truth, importance, usefulness, or interest value of any of the things one is engaged in . . ."

There are many variations on the theme, perhaps none of them with more weight than the view that the entire course of life on the earth shows no evidence of design or goal. A specialist in evolutionary theory writes: "Progress toward any goal . . . can no longer be considered as characteristic of evolution or even as inherent in it . . . man is the result of purposeless . . . process that did not have him in mind. He was not planned." [26]

For those who through faith or trust in the teachings of religion, through constitutional optimism or for whom the preoccupations of daily living are absorbed enough to have no time or concern for questions of this kind, further discussion will offer little of interest. Certainly not everyone would agree with Socrates that "the unexamined life is not worth living." The evidence, on the other hand, that an increasingly large number are troubled, depressed or anxious about the issues outlined is impressive enough to have provided the motive for the writing of this book.[A]

Many expressions of belief, mood and attitude similar to those above could be cited. They convey the image of a world bleak, cold; of a human existence insecure, tormented and forlorn. Such judgments cannot be brushed aside or taken lightly. Men of high competence have thought and felt in this way and have made fully clear the grounds of their philosophic postures. The grounds have been acknowledged even by those who disagree in interpretation.

There are many others, however, of equal competence in the same regions of thought who have emerged from explorations of the same data with quite different conclusions. They find evidence of a *plan* inherent in the processes of nature, and solid points of anchorage for faith in its design and purposiveness. They find grounds for the conviction that *despite its apparent cruelties there is a supremely meaningful ethical force at its roots*, as basic and real as any of the features that have made men doubt and despair. It is true that this faith requires some major changes in our conception of the *way* in which life has evolved, and of the *kind* of deity at work within it, but this means only that neither philosophy nor theology can remain fixed as our knowledge of the core processes of reality increase in depth.

To set forth this view and perspective, some findings in the fields of evolutionary biology, of interpretations of human history and of the "theology of nature" may now be examined.

CHAPTER 2

Meaning in Evolution

IN THE previous chapter some views of an evolutionist were quoted. They expressed the belief that the advent of man upon the earth was an accidental outcome of forces without direction, plan or purpose, any more than the number turned up when a dice is rolled is the result of a "plan" in the toss.

A biologist writes: "The hardest blow that Darwin struck against faith was not the proof that man had come from beasts, but the assumption that the whole evolutionary process depends finally on variations that arise by chance." [27] A great philosopher applied the same thought to the entire course of human existence. "Man is the product of causes which had no prevision of the end they were achieving; his origin, his growth, his hopes and fears, his loves and his beliefs, are but the outcome of accidental collocations of atoms." [24]

Here, surely, is something basic to the questions raised earlier. If the evolution of life itself has been without goal or purpose, some important deductions may be made regarding related issues. An individual may have personal goals, of course, but can his existence be said to have purpose in any deeper sense if the processes which evolved him are devoid of it?

Before the time of Darwin one of the strongest arguments for divine intelligence, foresight and benevolence was the evidence of *design* in all things created. Among examples were the striking fitness in the forms and functions of animals to the special features of their environments. The Wisdom was evident in the perfect physical adaptations to life in the sea, the desert or the Arctic. The patterning and precision of insect behavior, the "marvels of instinct," were among the many testimonials to the skill of the Creator.

With Darwin the entire picture changed. The image of the Master Designer vanished, to be replaced by a view of life in which every organism was a product of a prolonged and painful ordeal of trial and error. "Natural selection" (of the superior animal in the "struggle for existence") became the great designer, but of a very different kind. *This* one worked by experiment, mistaken starts and many failures. "Design" became not a well-planned construction but the end result of a process in which organisms survived because they *happened* to have assets of some sort that gave them an advantage in the competition for food and mates, and in the effort to escape enemies.*

---

* The natural selection theory, in summary, is that the enormous overproduction of offspring in nature entails severe pressures for food and living space. This pressure, along with need to avoid enemies, puts a premium on all individual differences which confer advantages affecting survival. When these differences are large, and transmitted to offspring, they are known as mutations. When the favored organisms reproduce more than the less fortunate over many generations, a new species may arise. *Selection*, by "nature," is a figure of speech meaning that, for the reasons given, some individuals reproduce more than others.

The word "happened" here means favored by chance, *lucky* because physically or mentally gifted in some way. Nature favors some organisms in size, strength, fleetness, acuteness of sense, in sexual attractiveness, fighting equipment or intelligence. All these are assets, but variations may also be defects and a liability. Variations are "blind" in the sense that they may or may not confer an advantage. It is as if nature were guessing, and guessing because there was no way of knowing.

The authority of Darwin himself favored this conclusion. "There seems no more design in the variability of organic beings," he wrote," than in the course which the wind blows." He appeared to be troubled about this conclusion, however, and inclined to see "designed laws" at work, basically, with only the details worked out by chance. Many would understand the mood in which he sensed "the impossibility of conceiving this immense and wonderful universe, including man with his capacity for looking far backwards and far into futurity, as the result of blind chance or necessity.[9]

Calling mutations *random* means that they are unrelated to the needs of the organism in its strivings for survival. It means that anything may happen as a mutation; that there is no apparent logic about their occurrence. Survival depends on the outcome of encounters with the environment and on whatever chance has supplied as equipment for coping with them.

Is this description of the process of evaluation final, or are there dissenting voices? There are respected professional students of evolution who are sure that it is inadequate, that in important respects it is false. They believe that a great many phenomena cannot be plausibly fitted to this doctrine for the origins of new forms of life.

The basic question is whether chance plus selection

will explain enough. If it does not, we will want to know at what point something more than chance is needed. Is there, in other words, evidence of an additional *guiding* factor that has influenced change in the direction which evolution has taken? This is the most fundamental problem of human and animal development. It is also a central problem among evolutionists. It is "the biology of ultimate concern."

It may be noted at outset that the all-important mutations are not limited to structures. They may begin with the *behavior* of the animal when this differs in certain ways from that of its species. When the new behavior spreads to others—assuming it is an improvement—those whose physical traits chance to favor it will be more likely to survive.

As a simple example a biologist describes the way in which flying fishes might evolve. We are asked to imagine a fish, in desperate flight from an enemy, leaping momentarily out of the water in its panic to escape. If successful, such behavior might certainly be repeated, and thus become a *habit*—"the habit of keeping themselves out of harm's way for as long as possible; and they would do this by skimming along the surface using the pectoral fins for support with the lower lobe of the tail vibrating in the water for propulsion, as does that close relative of the flying fish . . . sometimes called the skipper." [12]

The next step comes when, for certain individuals, mutations result in larger fins and a larger lobe to the tail. The fins, now more winglike, enable the fish to glide over the surface for greater distances. Finally a number of fish have become markedly changed because a new habit has favored—or "selected"—the physical traits which supported it.

Another example from the many possible concerns the

feeding behavior of birds. "If birds of a particular species, originally feeding on insects from the surface of the bark of trees, found, in a time of shortage, that they could get some prey by probing into or under the bark, then they might develop a change of habit which, by being copied by other members of this species, could gradually spread through the whole population." [13] Those birds which then *happen* to have beaks better shaped for probing under bark will in the long run be the likelier to survive and propagate. Thus a new beak form arises, selected by a behavior change out of changes in structure.

To account for behavior selected in this way it is assumed that *some* animals must be capable to a greater degree than others of departures from the usual ways of the species. Such departures are prompted by the need to survive. Yet new, *original* behavior may result, and from it, eventually, new species. At the higher levels of behavior such terms as "creative" and "purposive" may fittingly be used to describe it. It is, a biologist suggests, "the creativity that is inherent in every organism . . . the *inner* . . . directiveness, moving towards goals of many kinds and at many levels." [41]

In the lower animals such purposiveness may not be impressive, but it represents the beginnings of what in man merges into the highest forms of creative achievement. How far the selective principle alone can account for the varieties of human purposiveness will be examined later. The question at this point is whether there is evidence of an *inherent plan* in evolution. There are facts which are strongly suggestive.

There are structures in different species of animals which are similar owing to descent from a common ancestry. One of the favorite illustrations in books on biology pictures the bones of the human arm, the foreleg of a dog and the wing of a bird. Despite the differences, the likenesses in basic structure are easily seen. The differences are clearly adapted to the uses to which the members are put.

One might expect that such widely different functions as flying and walking would have led to basically different designs. What we find, however, are simply variations of the same pattern; a few original forms with minor changes. Considering the enormous variety of the world's environments and the endless variety of animal forms (over two million species) we might expect, if chance alone determined the mutations, a great number of different forms. What we find, instead, is a very small number.

The point becomes clearer when such basic similarities are found among species living in very unlike environments and representing independent lines of evolution. This is true, for example, of the two main branches of the mammals: those in which the growth of the young is completed within the maternal body and those in which it is terminated in an external pouch. Here is a great difference in reproductive method in two forms which were separated from their common ancestors for many millions of years. One group inhabited Australia when that continent was still a part of Asia, while the other failed to reach it before the separation of the two continents.

For over a hundred million years the two branches evolved in complete independence, yet the resulting types, compared species with species (moles, squirrels, the mouse-like jerboa, wolves) are strikingly similar in structures. There can be no question but that the basic body plans are the same. Can such similarities and *stability* be explained by assuming nothing more than the selective effect of environment along with entirely random individual variations? There must have been great changes of environment between the two continents over so enormous a span of time. One student of evolution has summarized the view of many, that it is "almost an absurdity" that such stability of forms could be the result of chance variation in view of the "great variety of environments which a single species may encounter and the variety of different kinds of animals which may live in the same habitat . . ."[11] This stability, he writes, "is absolutely fundamental to what we are talking about when we speak of evolution. Yet in truth we cannot explain it at all in terms of present-day biological theory."

Another example of the same kind is seen in the *method* by which one animal form is "shaped" into another in the course of evolution. If the major changes of animal forms are truly the summed-up effects of entirely random changes in the individual elements of the body, we could hardly expect any *overall* pattern or design to be maintained. The randomness should show in the independence of each small change of every other. One would expect, in other words, a chaotic kind of transformation, a disjointedness or incoordination.

But this is not at all what actually happens in evolutionary change. The parts of a pattern of change do not behave like the product of chance events. They are not independent of each other. They are related to each other in a definite way. Overall design is preserved throughout the change. In some instances it could even be said that each unit of change is mathematically predictable in relation to all the others. In a word, such changes are *systematic*—just the opposite of what would be expected if the underlying origins were governed by chance.*

* Similar observations have been made of that richly various complex: the human face. Here also the harmony of parts is a product of coordinated elements. In a face with a short forehead and large expanse from eyes to chin, for example, all the features will be correspondingly large.

Every animal trait is an outcome, according to selection theory, of the demands to which the environment subjects variations. All have been retained because of their tested values. They reflect the screening process by which they have been chosen for survival by nature's method of trial by ordeal.

Certain biologists have pointed out, however, that an organism may have capacities which cannot have arisen in this way because they are a response to stresses that do not occur in nature. They may be so unusual or abnormal that it is safe to assume that they never happened in the history of the species. Laboratory experiments have subjected organisms to highly artificial traumas.

One example involved a variety of sponges. The system of cells which compose it was completely disintegrated, first by mechanical crushing, then by forcing the resulting cell mass through the openings of a piece of cloth of fine mesh. The sponge tissues were thereby broken into single cells or small groups of cells.

The single cells then began to move, "sending out questing protoplasmic strands of filaments." The individual cells came together, one by one, to form clusters, which in turn merged into larger masses "not unlike the original body of which they all were once members." Finally they became specialized for different functions and eventually an *organized animal* was self-restored. "Like soldiers in a

---

The same correspondence holds when the features as a total pattern are small in relation to the size of the head. In another instance all features may exhibit a finely chiseled quality with well-defined moulding, or all will be coarse and crude, suggesting an unfinished sculpture.

Skeletal structures exhibit a similar phenomenon. "One of the most impressive experiences a student of evolution can have is to realize the extent to which all the smaller structural alterations of the human skull are correlated with and dependent upon each other and the extent to which they are governed by the trend of the skull formation as a whole." [36]

well-drilled military unit . . . they assembled in orderly formation. . . . How this is possible is a secret still locked in the innermost structure of protoplasm." [28] Here, in a very primitive form of life, was complex and coordinated behavior which could not have been "selected" in similar situations of the past, since no such stresses had ever before been encountered.*

Another example is provided by one of the countless experiments on the fruit fly. One of its mutations resulted in eyeless individuals. These were bred in such a way that the genes for normal vision were entirely eliminated. All the progeny would therefore be expected to be eyeless for an indefinite period. Yet flies with normal vision appeared in a few generations. That sheer coincidence could account for the almost immediate recovery of vision by restoring the eye-producing gene would surely be too much for even the "chance theory" of mutation. What is far more plausible is that the *system* of genes which coordinates the parts of the visual function included the capacity for self-repair after a damaging mutation. An event in one part of the system elicited events in other parts, all directed to the end of maintaining continuous vision.

That such *directed* change can result from chance mutations has been seriously questioned by a number of biologists. The evolution of new forms begins with change in the individual organism. Evidence of directedness here suggests that *comparable factors may be active in evolution as a whole.*

---

* One biologist finds it "difficult to believe" that the ability of organisms to regenerate lost parts can be explained by selection because of the rarity of such need in the natural course of life. "In nature there are few occasions when the ability of an isolated piece of stem to restore a root system . . . would be called upon." An organism's capacity to respond to certain kinds of experimental damage may have no parallel in nature, he thinks, or at any rate "could almost never have occurred." [29]

Among the phenomena of nature most familiar to the layman are the "marvels of instinct." Some of these have impressed biologists as well, not only as masterpieces of design but as challenges to the selection formula. The basic question is whether they can be satisfactorily fitted to the "chance theory."

In preface to a few examples it should be said that the problem is in part a question of sheer plausibility. Professionals often say that if we are to fully understand the selection theory we must never forget that the number of mutations and generations involved have been spread over a virtually unlimited span of time. No matter how hard it is to conceive of what could happen in a near-infinity of random events, we are assured that it did happen or *could* have happened, whether we can imagine it or not. Billions of years of geological history are a part of the earth's past, regardless of the fact that no human mind can possibly grasp such a period, any more than it can grasp the possibility—to use a favorite comparison—that a million monkeys with typewriters could by chance alone write a Shakespearean play if they kept at it *long* enough.

No such ordeal need be asked of the reader. The central question will be what choices remain if the idea of chance is rejected, or cannot be "tolerated"—as someone has put it. The alternatives must be more plausible and must not violate any fundamentals of biology.

The animal world exhibits many and various kinds of protective markings and coloration. The body may resemble a leaf, a twig or some other natural object—even a blob or splatter of excrement. Anything to deceive the enemy. According to theory such resemblances must begin with random alterations in appearance which *happen*, in some instances, to reproduce the patterns or colors of inanimate nature.

Animals fortunate enough to vary in these ways will tend to survive and to reproduce their variations. As these continue to accumulate in the same direction the advantage will increase until the maximum camouflage effect is achieved. Any changes which do not help will tend to be eliminated, since their bearers will be at a disadvantage.

The strain on plausibility may appear to be small when enormous periods of time are assumed for completion of the process. For some the strain may begin where protective patterns include extremely refined and minute detail in the matching of an animal with its background. Studies of birds, for example, are reported in which the very texture of the physical surroundings is matched, as well as the colors. Thus birds living on a finely grained soil will exhibit a highly uniform coloration, while those living on pebbly ground will have a correspondingly coarse-grained coloration pattern.

The strain becomes greater, however, when *behavior*, as well as visible pattern and color, is found to precisely match features of the environment. "We thus see many animals taking up special resting positions which will bring their camouflage pattern into the best relationship with the background upon which they are resting . . . for example . . . we see a hawk moth which has dark bands upon its wings that reproduce the shadows in the vertical cracks of the bark of a tree; it invariably rests with its head pointing upward so that the bands reproduce the background." [23] That this behavior is inborn is shown by the fact that the animal itself is unable to see the match between its own body and the environment.

Another case of "purposive design" is that of *mimicry*. Certain insects are avoided by preying animals because of their unpleasant taste. Their color patterns serve as warning signals for avoidance by predators. If, by accidental changes in appearance, a different kind of insect should begin to display patterns of color and line which happen to resemble those of the noxious variety, it would begin to benefit by the likeness. The better the imitation the greater the chance of survival. Successful mimicry depends on unlimited possibilities of such mutations of pattern, form and color.*

What are the actual products of a series of these "accidents in the right direction" like? The findings are among the most impressive of natural phenomena. The resemblances of even extremely elaborate patterns, of which hundreds have been observed, may be so close as to be described as "almost photographic" as duplications. Since mimicry has been observed in insects of entirely different orders, as when flies or beetles mimic bees or wasps, it is not surprising that the idea of "creation by accident" has seemed incredible even to some professionals. "So striking are the similarities of colour patterns between butterflies of different kinds that for a time many naturalists could not believe that they could be the product of selection." [14] The refinements of the selective process which must be assumed in order to account for such formation have been described as "fantastic." †

---

* An objection sometimes made to the selection principle at this point is that a variation in the right direction might *initially* be so small as to have little or no protective value, raising the question as to how it could be preserved as a base for additional changes which *would* begin to have such value. A large mutation toward a complex pattern, on the other hand, would raise another question, since the larger the advance the less the probability it could occur as a random mutation.

† It would be of interest to know how many biologists have entertained such doubts and have been reticent of expressing them against the "right-wing," two-factor doctrine of evolution. The situation may be comparable to that of the psychologists who may have misgivings about the current trend to explain almost everything about human behavior in terms of the learning process with small allowance for the role of genetics.

In another type of imitative mutation a flower spontaneously changes in structure, color and odor, causing it to resemble so closely the females of certain insects that the males of the species are sexually attracted to make contact with the flower for the reproductive act, depositing the pollen which serves the procreatives needs of the plant. The selection theory requires us to suppose that this subtle and purposeful tricking of an animal by a plant has come about through an accumulation of accidental changes in plant anatomy and physiology.

A further remarkable challenge for the random mutation formula has been reported in a case of protective mimicry in which, through inherited individual variations in color, a swarm of flying insects coordinates its behavior to compose, when distributed upon a dead twig, an integrated pattern resembling a flower—an "insect flower"—this being a created form, not duplicating any other found in nature. Here we are to suppose that, in a multitude of insects, *each* varied, and by chance, in a way such that *together* they composed an organized and meaningful figure.

*   *   *

Passing from examples of physical form to those of animal behavior leads into a region with which most people with any interest have some familiarity and which may therefore be briefly described. The facts, however, are fully as difficult for the doctrine of selection. A great variety of examples of inborn animal behavior are available to represent the problem.

One case for the purpose is that of the "trap-door" spider.[16] This creature attaches delicately slender leaves to the margins of its burrow so that the passing prey, by contact with a leaf, communicates its presence by the vibration. The arrangement of the leaves, systematically positioned for every direction of approach, informs the spider of the exact location of its victim in advance of its attack. A biologist comments that this "and many other examples of elaborate instinctive patterns must in the first place have arisen by new habits being . . . passed into the instinctive equipment . . ." Selection theory supposes that sheer accidents of mutation in the animal's nervous system coincided exactly with the new habits and were perpetuated as inborn behavior. The complexity and precision of organization in such behavior would appear to be even greater than that of the refined patterning of line and texture in protective camouflage and in mimicry.

Another example is supplied by Konrad Lorenz.[19] A bird reared in an enclosure, making it impossible for it to either fly or gain any visual experience of distances, is able, nonetheless, at the moment of leaving the nest, to "judge" spatial relationships accurately and to cope "in its rapid flight, with all the intricacies of air resistance, upcurrents, turbulence, and air pockets." What the bird "knows," in this instance, in thus reacting to its environment without previous experience, "would fill many volumes." Description of the inborn skills in space perception required for such performances would occupy "whole textbooks of stereometry, and that of the responses and activities of flying, an equal number . . . on aerodynamics.*

---

* Attention has been called to certain highly specific challenges to the concept of random mutation.[18] The African warthog exhibits callosities on its forelegs, on which it leans while feeding. The ostrich has two "bulbous thickenings" on its legs, "one fore, one aft," on which it rests. These formations are present in the embryo as inherited characters. A student queries: "Is it conceivable that these callosities should have evolved by chance . . . just exactly where the animal needed them?" It is difficult to believe that developments so sharply focused upon the animal's needs could be wholly undirected, despite our ignorance as to the way in which a directive agency might operate.

The same logic would apply to the "very realistic false eyes" on the *back* of the head of certain birds (owls, kingfishers) as a means of reducing the threat of attack from the rear.

A final example may be taken from the behavior of birds in sounding alarm to the flock when danger threatens. The k*ind* of call is vital in this instance, since it places the caller himself in jeopardy by revealing his whereabouts. It must be one which will reach all concerned but whose source will be hard to find.

In one species it is "a high, thin, drawn-out whistling call." An analyst has pointed out that this is precisely the kind of sound which is most difficult to localize. "If a sound begins and ends gradually, with no sudden breaks or changes in loudness, the difference in times of arrival to each of the listener's ears will be difficult to determine . . ." and thus the location of the source.* If the pitch is high and pure, moreover, the difference in arrival time of the air waves in striking each ear will be further reduced, and thus the direction of the source more difficult to fix. This extremely delicate adjustment, according to selection theory, was evolved out of entirely random "experiments" in behavior.

*   *   *

A biologist has offered a helpful illustration of the meaning of evolution as a process in which selection is made, out of directionless variations and over enormous time periods, of just those which best serve the needs of adaptation.[6] Imagine, he suggests, that "billions of blind painters each sprinkle a few splashes of colour on millions of canvases. Of these, only the few that show the feeblest suggestion of a meaningful picture are preserved; the rest are destroyed. The selected rudimentary pictures are reproduced a millionfold. Again millions of blind painters add a few random touches of paint here and there. Again

* Marler, P. R. "The Drive to Survive." In *Animal Behavior.* The National Geographic Society, 1972, pp. 40–41.

the best pictures are selected and reproduced, and so on millions of times, corresponding to the number of generations that have elapsed since life began."

A new animal structure or capacity begins, according to theory, as no more than a crude sketch of what it is finally to become. It is a simple and primitive foreshadowing, full of imperfections. The final product will be far better fitted to adapt the organism to the demands of the environment. The "random touches of paint" are, of course, the mutations. The eliminated paintings represent the organisms which fail to adapt well enough to survive. What survives must prove itself over vast epochs of time, in competition with others amid the stresses of a changing milieu and the threats of enemies. Clearly such a method means colossal waste and, like all creative efforts, the risk of failure. But with an enormous potential of variations and rigorous elimination of unfavorable ones over unimaginable spans of time, organisms minutely adapted could, according to theory, finally emerge.[A]

The considerations so far reviewed have involved mainly a strain on credulity. There are others which offer logical difficulties as well.

Highly developed human capacities must be products of a long evolutionary process. For those with clear survival value there may be no problem. But how account for those for which such value appears to be lacking? Certain abilities are commonly prized for what they add to life as a kind of bonus, rather than for their utility. The appreciation of natural beauty would be one example. While highly regarded as an esthetic pleasure it cannot be classed with the equipment needed by primitive man in coping with the rigors and demands of the early world. It is not evident how it would confer an advantage in the struggle and competition for survival.

The same question may be asked about the capacity for *creation* in the realm of esthetics. Among the most complex of human abilities are those expressed in the great masterpieces of art: the sculpture of Michelangelo, the paintings of Rubens, the symphonies of Beethoven and the poetry of Shakespeare. Evolutionary developments of vast duration must be assumed, but it is not evident what selective processes kept them going and continuously refined them. For the beginnings of a civilized society some case might perhaps be made, but not for the immeasurably longer eons of prehistory when survival demands were severe and when utility was by far the most vital factor. A biologist writes: "There is a wide range of behavior . . . which cannot be reduced to utilitarian principles of adaptation of the individual and survival of the species. Greek sculpture, Renaissance painting, German music . . . have nothing to do with utility, or with the better survival of individuals or nations." * [2]

Few human abilities are now of greater value as tools of man's mastery of nature than mathematics, and no form of genius is more impressive than that seen in such men as Archimedes, Newton and Gauss, but if we are to view this highly complex gift as the final product of vast natural-selective labors it must be asked what advantage its rudimentary beginnings gave to man of a hundred millennia ago, and what conditions continued to develop and refine it.

Some human capacities have no apparent utility in the

---

* An anthropologist writes:

A hint of the esthetic sense or something very close to it is found in early Acheulian times, in occasional hand axes shaped far more beautifully than required for strictly utilitarian purposes. Such pieces may represent pride of craftsmanship more than art, but they show that man was expressing feelings for proportion and symmetry several hundred thousand years ago.[23]

ordinary conditions of life, either primitive or modern. Thus, the draftsmanship of a great artist; the manual dexterity of a concert pianist; the sense of balance of a tightwire acrobat; the mental skills of a master chess player. That these refinements of function are to be seen as products of undirected mutation which have not yet encountered the survival demands for which they have adaptive value leaves unanswered the question as to the selective processes by which they arrived at their present status.*

It has been questioned whether changes of environment alone, along with random mutations, could have brought about the enormous increase in the sheer *complexity* of organisms from the single cell to man. Professor Whitehead, among others, has argued that the need to adjust to environment cannot explain "the fact that organic species have been produced from inorganic . . . matter, and the fact that in the lapse of time organic species of higher and higher types have evolved." † (A) [37] Man has traits which are unique, and we must ask what *kind* of shifting of conditions of his life on earth could create this uniqueness out of the accidents of variation. Such questions

---

* "Some leading biologists still think that the evolution of the brain can never be accounted for in biological terms . . . that human mental potentialities have run ahead of any considerable needs or influences of natural selection, and that the aptitudes and facilities of the human brain are far in excess of what 'on any even remotely plausible view' would have been needed at any given point in evolution." [5]

† Teilhard de Chardin has made the same observation, with the question: "How do you explain this property of Natural Selection—that it persistently gives rise to . . . varieties more highly organized. . . . Can it be by accident that the *Weltstoff* . . . makes us . . . rise, taking advantage of every chance, to the level of a greater complexity . . . ?" [34]

Without internal directive factors, he believes, the form of life would have simply *varied* and *spread*; they would not have ascended to progressively higher psychological levels.

must be answered if we are to understand how a "living molecule" could evolve into a being capable of releasing nuclear energy and of traveling about the solar system.

Man's exploratory urge, his desire to understand, his curiosity, are fully meaningful in terms of the selection formula. They are basic to all that science has accomplished in control over nature and they have led to the most successful of all his adaptations. But what of his sense of wonder, of awe and mystery in contemplation of the universe, his perennial craving to discover a purpose in his being here. Man, as Albert Schweitzer once put it, "does not simply accept his existence as something given, but experiences it as something unfathomably mysterious." [25] Why does he not, like the lower animals, take his existence for granted and devote himself exclusively to satisfying his basic needs? What good does it do him, by the touchstone of natural selection, to torment himself with questions so difficult to answer, and which appear to be needless in relation to his adaptive goals?

Here, of course, we are on the margin of the "biological meaning" of religion, and the question of how it is to be fitted to the selection theory by aiding man in his struggle for increasingly effective living. There has never been a people without some form of religious attitude toward the world. A philosophical biologist has admitted it as difficult, "perhaps quite impossible," to explain how such emotions as reverence and piety has arisen in evolution.[(A) 9]

Human morale and confidence have been heightened by faith in the ultimate purposiveness of existence and the conviction that an overseeing divinity is on man's side in his strivings for ethically sanctioned goals. So far, on the other hand, as religion has been oriented toward the supernatural in a way tending to diminish or weaken the impulse to grasp and reshape the things of earth that need changing, the judgment, in the view of many, must go against it.

* * *

A number of fields of evidence have been reviewed for their bearing on the selection theory. The remarkable stability of the basic forms, the response to nonnatural stresses, the interaction of genes to maintain organ function (the eyeless fly), protective camouflage and mimicry, highly complex unlearned behavior in animals, and finally, human capacities which have developed to an extraordinary stature and degree of refinement in the apparent absence of selective processing have all been cited by professional biologists as serious problems for Darwinian theory. All are strongly suggestive of a *directive agency other than natural selection combined with chance.*

The random factor in mutations cannot be questioned; the data is copious and convincing. The central question is whether there are any checks at all on pure chance. Are the possibilities of variation entirely without limit or guidance? Is there evidence of a kind of selective factor entirely different from that imposed by the environment?

At this point the question must be widened to include *not only the origin of new forms of life but of life itself.* Before there was change from one form into another there was change from the nonliving to the living. If chance mutation with selection can account for the evolution of higher forms from lower, are we to suppose that chance events created a living organism at outset? Did the most complex of all creatures evolve from what were at first no more than accidents among the processes of lifeless physical nature?

Here we are at the level of physics and chemistry,

where professionals at once inform us that there are *laws* in both fields. A biochemist writes: "As in biological evolution itself, the formation and development of living from non-living matter cannot be attributed to the operation of 'pure chance.' It was by the operation of natural law that life arose . . ." There was potential within non-living matter, not only to evolve life but increasingly higher levels of organization.[22]

A biologist states, with reference to the theory of selection and of the origin of life by chance formations: "Selection, competition and 'survival of the fittest' already *presuppose* the existence of self-maintaining systems; they therefore cannot be the *result* of selection." No physical law is known, he continues, which would bring these systems out of a random state of organic matter. "And even if such systems are accepted as being 'given,' there is no law in physics stating that their evolution . . . would proceed in the direction of increasing organization . . ."[3]

Another writes: "Variation . . . follows chemical and biological laws. . . . There is no need to suppose that these laws, any more than those of biochemistry, are products of natural selection."[10] Again: "Evolution appears to be not a series of accidents, the course of which is determined only by the change of environments during earth history and the resulting struggle for existence . . . but is governed by definite laws . . ."[5]

The environment selects, but only after internal factors have screened a new creation out of many other possibilities. The origin of mutations is thus quite beyond the scope of natural selection, yet *all that makes man unique among animals has come from this source.*

* * *

In many primitive organisms (plants, sponges, slime molds) examples of behavior suggestive of "purposiveness" have been reported. The term has seemed proper because of their spectacular versatility in fulfilling the goals of development despite thwarting, damage and even severely destructive treatment of a kind never encountered in the normal course of life. A biologist who has vividly described such phenomena is sure that there is "inherent in the living system a . . . quality that keeps it directed toward a definite norm or course." [30] This is as true of behavior as of physical form. "Goal-seeking and directedness in organisms should be recognized as a basic fact and life's most characteristic quality." [31] The purposiveness seen in the growth of an organism *appears to be the same in kind* as the goal-seeking behavior of both man and animal.

A majority of biologists, according to Waddington, believes that "it is possible to discover a pattern in evolution as a whole—a general direction in which the process has proceeded." Human evolution has been more than "a mere contingent set of happenings which might equally well have taken a different form." [35] Not only, he believes, has there been an overall progressive movement; this directedness is not accidental; it is an outcome "of the general structure of the universe"—an inevitable product of the nature of the evolutionary processes.

A basic theme of evolution is that man, in a deeply fundamental sense, is a part of nature, that his origins lie in the animal world and that there has been *continuity* of development as one species gradually changed into another. No line can be drawn where consciousness or intelligence first arose. *Nor can a boundary be marked at which purposive behavior began as an entirely new event out of what had been devoid of goal seeking.* We may need to accept "that concepts of anticipation, purpose, and mind can be extended far down the scale of life." [1]

If, from a single cell, a human organism comes into being in whom consciousness and purposiveness are active, then something corresponding must have existed from the beginning. And since evolution is, in essence, an infinitely long series of individual developments, the same forces must be at work in both.

* * *

Purposiveness at the subhuman level is expressed in a variety of ways, some unlearned, some learned. In man it is through the medium of *culture*, meaning everything that one generation learns or inherits from those that have preceded it. The turn from biological to social inheritance was an enormously important one in evolution. Behavior came to be shaped mainly by socially transmitted knowledge, skills and influences. Social inheritance made possible a vast accumulation. It also greatly increased the rate of change.

When an historian wrote that the laws of biology provide a key to history he had in mind mainly the effect of individual differences upon its events and trends. The response of the individual to society has been a potent force in history when he changes it more than he is affected by it, and thus becomes a creative factor.

Evolution has become mainly cultural, but what culture transmits began with someone's experience; originality is an individual phenomenon. All cultures are expressed by the individual, and if they cannot entirely account for his behavior he must be seen as in some way or degree a biological *variant*. Culture, a psychologist writes, does not create a human being. "It doesn't implant within him the ability . . . to be creative. Rather it permits . . . or fosters, or encourages . . . what exists in embryo to become real and actual. . . . The culture is sun and food and water; it is not the seed." [20] Individuality has a role in cultural origins; in that of religion, for example. "The very beginning, the intrinsic core, the . . . universal nucleus of every known high religion . . . has been the private, lonely, personal illumination, revelation, or ecstacy of some acutely sensitive prophet or seer." [21]

In the conforming person the effects of environment are most clearly seen. In the eccentric or deviant the unlearned differences are more evident. In "genius" when expressed in creativity, they are at maximum. Purposiveness may lie in this fundamental trend toward originality or creativeness. Some recent philosophies—as will later be seen—identify deity itself with creativeness. As the biologist views it, it is usually thought of as organic change from which new species arise, but it includes behavior, both animal and human. "From the synthesis of a new substance by an organism, or the origin of new species, to supreme creation in the imagination of an artist or a poet, we are dealing with the same restless, changeful, trailblazing quality of life . . ." [32]

What form does a *psychological* "mutation" take? It must be in some way a departure from custom, from conformity, the "normal." It will be found, not among those whose behavior can be understood as a social product, but in the domain of the mental frontiersman who revolts against some feature of his environment and perhaps changes it.

One of the more insightful psychologists among the major biographers has made some suggestions in his treatment of the *daimonic*. This is "the unrest that is in all of us, driving each of us out of himself"—out, that is, of his habitual self. It is something primordial, deeply implanted, which impels toward departures from established patterns and toward exploratory ventures; "unpathed waters, undreamed of shores." [38] In most people, he suggests, it is negligibly small, expressed only rarely in a brief longing to escape from the worn channels of habit and commonplaces.

More significant is the daimonic impulse in its major forms. The basic unrest then becomes chronic, insistent and compelling. It is an urge to transcend boundaries; it is inquiring, adventurous, even danger-seeking. Whatever its direction or form, its herald is a restlessness, a thrust against the bars of habit.

For Stefan Zweig, the outstanding symbol of this revolt is the creative artist, most vividly seen in genius. It is the character of achievement, however, rather than its stature that makes it truly creative. The daimonic is inspired, "derives from the unknown, from a region outside the domain of the waking conscious." Much biographical material illustrates the view of creative activity as compulsive in character. "A creative person has little power over his own life," wrote Carl Jung. "He is not free. He is captive and driven by his daimon."

What, finally, can we believe about evolution with regard to the issue of "plan versus chance"?

Human traits without apparent adaptive usefulness are among the many evidences of an internal directive agency in evolution. They are complex, highly developed and refined. Creativity and sensibility in the realms of art have been suggested examples. Some would include deep and intense nonsexual attachments between unrelated individuals, and some would add man's capacity for self-awareness, certain kinds of imagination, the sense of humor and the ability to laugh.

Such findings support the belief in purposiveness in evolution. They suggest an agency that guides though it does not fully control them. That the process has been cruel and wasteful, that it has entered blind alleys and has left many failures in its wake, clearly implies a different mode of creation than that of orthodox religion.

The essential processes of evolution center upon the individual. Evolutionary change occurs in a sequence of individuals. Variation is an individual phenomenon. Creative developments are always expressed in individual form. Planless variation in evolution is not in harmony with the fact of purposiveness in the individual life. An evolutionist who queries, "Did Beethoven create the Eroica by chance . . . ?" makes the significant comment that evolution resembles human creativity far more than a game of roulette.[A]

What is the directive factor in evolution if chance and selection are not enough?

There are laws at the deepest level of the processes which created life and which determined the events that followed. There is evidence of *organization* in these processes. It therefore seems not only permissible but necessary to believe that there is a plan at the core of evolution. It includes *both* directedness and random events. "Nature," writes a philosopher of science, "is ruled by laws of cause and laws of chance in a certain mixture." [7] Another, who also sees the world as a mixture of chance and order, states that the "universality of order and of creative freedom *from* order are two expressions of the immanence of God . . ." [17] The method of the plan includes improvisation, trial and error, "groping" and "opportunism." *A design with built-in orientation may proceed experimentally, in this sense, and still be called a plan.*

A large question remains for a later chapter: How to fit such findings to a comprehensible and acceptable image of deity.

CHAPTER 3

Evolution and Ethics

ONE of the subjects reported in our first chapter was appalled when he realized that predatory behavior in the animal world is "neither accidental nor immoral." By accidental he meant a nonintentional defect, as in a child born deformed. By immoral he meant "wrong in the sight of God." The order of predator and prey is clearly inherent in nature, with divine sanction implied.

For some of the many who have been assailed by religious doubt, a conflict of this kind may be full of meaning, and even vital. If there is "evil" rooted at the core of nature, how is it to be reconciled with certain teachings of the Church as to the moral responsibility of mankind? The true origin of "original sin" may be in question.

During a therapy-group discussion on religious issues a young woman expressed herself as follows:

I have a nine-year-old cousin who has been a great problem. He is always in trouble with other children. He is very rough with them, beating them up and taking things that belong to them. He steals from his mother's purse. He likes to torment dogs and cats and nearly killed a pet canary.

None of his brothers and sisters are anything like him. A children's psychiatrist spent a lot of time with him and said he was a "sociopathic personality" and that it was constitutional. It was like being a mental defective except that it was his emotions instead of his intelligence. He said there have always been people like this, meaning a lot of adults too.

I've thought about this a great deal. This boy is certainly "wicked" if the word means anything, but if the psychiatrist is right, how are we supposed to think about such things; I mean about sin and guilt, if this boy can't help himself.

In a similar vein a forty-two-year-old male spoke briefly of a discussion with the minister of the Baptist church to which he belonged: "This minister has a kind of habit of talking about our 'lower nature' and our 'higher nature,' and that one is divine and the other is the animal part of man. He says God wants us to overcome this part, but I get confused. If God created the animal world, how can we think of the part of us that came from it as wrong or sinful?"

These statements clearly relate to problems outlined in Chapter I. They raise a basic question which must at times inevitably trouble a thoughtful person—or so it would seem—whose perceptions have not been blinded by dogma: that of the *ethical structure of the world.*

The issue is well defined in the framework of evolutionary theory. The "order of nature has a code of its own, seen quite clearly in nature's arenas. Superior strength and ruthlessness is favored for survival and propagation." Superiority of this kind is a "virtue" and may be regarded as a base of an ethic. One of the nineteenth-century deductions was "social Darwinism"—the thesis that, for example, uncontrolled competition and self-interest in commercial contest and conquest is approved by nature herself, and so must be morally beyond question.

That such a view did not follow was apparent when it was seen that natural selection also applies when one *group* competes with another, and that cooperation and mutual aid among the members would have survival value. "Not only individuals but . . . tribes and races, are units of natural selection . . . evolutionary processes may promote the formation of codes of ethics which . . . operate against the interests of a few individuals but which favor the group to which these individuals belong. Among . . . social insects, an individual often sacrifices its life for the sake of the colony." [10]

The fact remains that exploitation is an essential of nature's economy and that it is in conflict with a different kind of ethics which holds it evil for the strong to deprive the weak, and wrong for anyone to *use* another solely for his own ends. For some this means that the predominant code of the animal world must be rejected for human behavior. A great evolutionist wrote: "Let us understand, once for all, that the ethical progress of society depends not on imitating the cosmic process . . . but in combating it." [16] By human and humane standards a reversal of this feature of animal behavior is imperative: instead of victimizing others, to respect their needs and give them aid; instead of selfish aggression, to acknowledge the rights of others and to restrain many of one's "natural urges."

An exhortation to "combat the cosmic process" certainly implies that conflict is deeply inherent in nature, and in man, if he is part of nature.

A specialist in evolutionary theory who rejects the "tooth-and-claw" principle of competition concedes that if there is to be a *natural* ethics it must be sought within the data of nature herself. He proposes that the development of individuality is a fundamental feature of evolution. Under the name of variation it is most in evidence at the higher levels of animal life. From this it is possible to derive an ethic—that it is "good, right, and moral . . . to promote the realization or fulfillment of individual capacities. It is bad, wrong, and immoral . . . to impede such fulfillment." [22] Another evolutionist agrees: "Anything which permits or promotes open development is right; anything which frustrates development is wrong." [17] It follows, too, that while expression of individuality is good, limits must be set in the interests of social harmony and in recognition of the rights of each person. Such rights must not be invaded; "it is wrong to develop one individual at the expense of another."

If a code of this kind could be derived from the fact of individuality it would seem to warrant regard as *natural*. Yet individual differences include superior and inferior abilities, and therefore unequal power to achieve goals. It may be wrong for the strong to exploit the weak, but history as well as biology supports this exploitation, illustrated in wars of conquest without number and the record of economic competitions which parallel those of the animal world.

In the interests of justice the position has been taken that everyone should have an equal chance to achieve individuality even though nature herself may not favor this code. Despite the enormous range of differences in ability there is one way or sense in which all are equal, and from which it follows that each must have the same right to achieve his goals. The hopes, frustrations and gratifications of the ungifted or inferior man are as important to him as are the like experiences of those who may excel him in every other way. Differences in capacity for happiness are much smaller than differences in ability. Grief and joy, for all we know, are closely comparable emotions in the genius, the average man, and in those much less than average.

Here then is a possible foundation for an ethics. There is question, however, not so much about its truth as to how far such an abstraction can influence behavior. Such a code clearly needs a supporting motive. If it is to offset the drive to exploit, it must have comparable strength, and if it is to overcome this drive it must be potentially stronger.

While I may acknowledge the rights of another to express his individuality, my treatment of him is not likely to be affected unless I also *care* about him. Otherwise, with my own desires active, I will hardly be checked by thoughts of what is due him, or about an evolutionary trend toward individuality. Here, as so often elsewhere, emotion is more potent than codes.* Does evolution provide a basis for ethics in the sentiment of *concern* for others?

Many millions of years ago something new and of enormous significance entered the animal world. With the emergence of the mammals the newborn young came into life in a helpless state, requiring nurturing and protective maternal care. To meet this need a corresponding impulse

---

* A sociologist writes: "Neither the sublime actions of love nor the ethics of reverence for life can be . . . motivated by purely rational . . . thought." [23] William James observed: "If your heart does not *want* a world of moral reality, your head will assuredly never make you believe in one." Konrad Lorenz: "If it were not for a rich endowment of social instincts, man could never have risen above the animal world . . . even the fullest rational insight into the consequences of an action . . . would not result in . . . a prohibition, were it not for some emotional . . . sources of energy supplying motivation." (Lorenz, K. *On Aggression.* New York: Bantam Books, Inc., 1967, p. 238.)

or instinct evolved and a distinctive kind of emotion could be inferred.

Mankind being mammalian, the emotion is now directly known. It is among the most powerful of urges, most commonly called maternal love—in essence, the urge to respond to the needs of another creature. A basic thesis in this region of behavior is that impulses of this kind "are one and all derivatives of the maternal instinct and products of female evolution. . . . Maternal affection . . . is the original source of love." [13]

The parental relationship among mammals is essentially that of mother and offspring, the paternal role being small. One student has suggested that solicitude gradually developed in the female's response to her mate, the process being part of "the psychological evolution of the female, and it appears probable that in the human species love was at first confined to woman." The capacity for maternal feeling was finally transmitted far beyond it. "Just as the transferred affection of the female for the male is a derivative of maternal love, so likewise *all* feelings of a tender, compassionate, altruistic character . . . are extensions and transformations of the maternal instinct and are directly derived from it." [9]

In the same vein it has been proposed that the *humane* impulses of the human female, as part of her maternal nature, lie deep in human origins and are the root of all that followed in the same direction. "The love of a mother for her child is the basic patent and model for all human relationships. Indeed, to the degree to which men approximate in their relationships with their fellow men the love of the mother for her child, to that extent do they move more closely toward the attainment of perfect human relations." [20] Love itself, as Ashley Montagu defines it, is precisely the feeling of responsiveness to others, the impulse to support, to minister to the needs of others because one is *emotionally involved* in their needs.[21]

Definitions of love in terms of tenderness, solicitude and compassion have given to the word by far its most common meaning. It centers upon the needs of its object; it is "self-offering and self-spending"—in essence, self-giving. It desires, not possession, but the well-being of the beloved; it is prompted to sacrifice and self-denial. Its response is independent, to a greater degree than in any other human relationship, of the qualities and merits of the person loved.

Henri Amiel's description of himself is apt in this context. "It is my nature to be caressing . . . compassionate, sympathetic, to abandon myself to the collective life, to seek to make animals and men happy, to be kind to all creatures, helpful to every living thing. . . . But these are the paternal and conjugal qualities, so I am not unworthy to be a husband and father."[1]

The resemblance, if not identity, of the quality and power of "compassionate," "benevolent" and "altruistic" emotion in the love for an unrelated person and that of parent for child is illustrated in the following testimonials, the first expressing a mother-son relationship, the second that of a man for an "unrelated" person—his wife. They are intended only to give concreteness to the discussion.

I often have to fight against the impulse to do more than I should for my son. I know I must allow him to develop his own resources and to become independent of me. I know it is necessary for him to experience stresses and disappointments if he is to mature.

But at times my love for him and my intense desire for his happiness grow so strong that it is almost more than I can cope with. It nearly overcomes me, so that I want to do things for him that I know I should not do. There are times when I am overwhelmed with a desire to make him completely happy. There is no sacrifice I would not make. At these times I feel that I want to give him everything that life can offer, even if it meant leaving myself nothing at all. I could accept destitution. I could even welcome it, if I knew it would contribute to his happiness.

A man in his sixties, married for twenty-five years, expressed intense feeling about the strength of the marital bond during a period when the loss of his wife was threatened by illness.

I've always heard that self-preservation is the strongest of all human instincts. I can say for myself that this is simply not true. I'm quite certain that if it were necessary I would give my life for my wife's well-being. I am also certain that there is no ordeal of pain, physical or mental, that I would not endure for her sake. The threat of losing her has made me realize more than ever before that my love for her is the greatest force in my life.

While I have a strong need of her as part of my life I believe that my desire for her well-being is greater. I once tried to analyze this and decided that I could even give her up entirely if for some reason it was the only way I could make her happy. To be apart from her and know she was happy would be preferable to having her with me if she were suffering.

The parallel emotional states are noted here only to stress the fact that if the parental bond is truly the source of those which may form outside the family, its radiation far beyond its point of origin is one of the supremely important realities.

It has been proposed that the root of a natural ethics may be found in the emotion that marked a turning point in the evolutionary process. A biologist (Simpson) has contrasted the "old evolution," prehuman and without awareness of good and evil, with the "new evolution," limited to mankind. The former was outside of morality; we cannot call it "evil" when a predatory animal kills its prey. The only ethics must therefore be human ethics; "in man a new form of evolution begins." It must be added, however, that while a *formulated* ethics is entirely human, the emotion by which it alone can become effective is far older than mankind. It began with response to the needs of the newborn.

Judgments have varied as to the most important advance in human evolution. The beginnings of the use of tools, the origin of speech, the emergence of conceptual thought have all been regarded as the outstanding advances of the "immense journey." There is fair agreement that the greatest step in *moral* evolution was the beginning of awareness of and concern for the needs of those beyond the family circle. It was at this point, too, that there began the most basic of human conflicts: the clash between the urge to exploit another as means to an end, and the impulse to respond to him not as an object, but as a *being* capable, as one's self, of experiencing needs, frustrations and distresses. Both elements are deep in the human makeup; the disharmony is within the structure of nature.[A]

This ethical conflict as *inherent* in the natural order relates closely to one of the basic issues outlined in Chapter 1. It is a vital element in the new theologies to be later reviewed, and no statement of the problem of evil is complete without it. The compassionate response to suffering in the animal world—as for the victim of a predator—is one symbol of the disharmony, the conflict being within (our given) nature, and so entirely by-passes the sphere of "free will" and "original sin."

A student of the history of the impulse, animal and

human, to meet the needs of others has proposed that the factor of "mutual aid" has been at least as important as competition in the evolution of behavior.[18] Among gregarious animals there is copious evidence of an instinctive parallel to the human social response. "Well-certified" instances of *compassionate* behavior are cited. While granting the wide prevalence of competition in the animal world, the vast amount of gregariousness "would be utterly impossible without a corresponding development of social feelings." [19]

Dobzhansky observes that while altruism assumes conscious choice, there are "countless examples" among the lower organisms of "members of a herd or flock . . . interposing themselves between a predator and the weaker . . . members." [13] Sorokin cites "an enormous body of evidence . . . showing that the principle of cooperation has possibly been even more important in the evolutionary process than that of egoistic struggle for existence . . . mutual aid in various forms is found . . . among all species, *especially among those that have to nurture their offspring*." [24]

How in human prehistory the change came about from emotional indifference to those outside the family to degrees of sympathetic participation in the lives of those beyond it may never be known. The moral pioneers, like the first toolmakers, astronomers and mathematicians, must be forever nameless. The usual individual variations may be surmized; in some the capacity was greater than in others. Differences in emotional temperament have been recorded down the centuries, illustrated, for example, in those who have enjoyed public executions and those who found them too painful to endure.

Historians of European society trace our science to the classical Greeks and our religious and ethical culture to the ancient Hebrews. An Egyptologist has suggested an earlier origin of the latter.

Long before the Biblical "age of revelation" and more than two thousand years before the beginnings of Hebrew history, the foundations of a moral code which included the concepts of righteousness and justice were formulated in Egypt. In this "great transformation," as Professor Breasted calls it, mankind for the first time—so far as the past is known to us—began to develop a moral sense, or concern for the rights of others. He quotes, from sources dating from the twenty-seventh to the twenty-second centuries B.C., maxims having some of the familiar flavor of Biblical exhortations.[5]

More acceptable is the virtue of the upright man than the ox of him that doeth iniquity.

Righteousness is for eternity. It descendeth with him that doeth it into the grave, . . . his name is not effaced on earth, but he is remembered because of right.

Established is the man whose standard is righteousness, who walketh according to its way.

A man's virtue is his monument, but forgotten is the man of evil repute.

The social and moral development of the society that grew up in the Nile valley contributed much, according to Breasted, to the Hebrew literature we know as the Old Testament. Our moral heritage comes in part "from a *human* past enormously older than the Hebrews, and it has come to us rather *through* the Hebrews than from them." [7] The ethical innovations of the Egyptian moralists arose from experiences within society; they were "not projected from the outside . . . by some mystic process called inspiration or revelation." It was the dawn of the "age of conscience" after millennia in which, so far as is known, nothing of its kind ever reached the dimension that could be called a social movement or major force. Breasted defines this great transformation, this slow birth of ethics, as *"the greatest discovery in the whole sweep of the evolutionary process as far as is known to us."* [7]

With Christianity there came a further phase. For biological evolution the individual is expendable; the species has priority. Vast numbers must finally fail to survive; the "runt of the litter" does not count. The new religion rejected this view as it rejected the cruelty of the exploitative design. It insisted, "century after century . . . upon the infinite worth of the individual human soul." It was as if, deep within the creative core of the evolutionary process, a reversal of course had occurred.

In the literature of ethics two major systems are outstanding. In one, virtue is equated to power, and all that aids the rule of the strong wins the mark of merit. What is good, always and everywhere is that which wins, dominates or at least survives. In the other, the central themes are charity, justice in all dealings, mercy and the value of the individual. In the Christian exhortation to neighborly goodwill it is made clear that one's neighbor is anyone in need, regardless of clan, tribe or race.

The correspondence between the two doctrines and the two phases of evolutionary trend is evident; likewise the basic opposition.

Philosophers among the biologists have applied nature's higher valuation of the species over the individual to the issue of purposiveness. The essence of evolution being its creativeness, only the creative individual is of worth in advancing the species. Uncountable multitudes, human and animal, must live outside of purposive trends. The uncreative masses are expendable, devoid of function except that there must be many, biologically, for the production of the few. They exist only as means; they are dross in the cosmic design, and must often be sacrificed. "The welfare of the species is paid for by the misery of many individuals."

In sharp conflict with this view, and equally rooted in biology, is the emotionally grounded rejection of such a design. Expressed in both Christian and "natural" ethics, it gives a fundamentally different status to the individual.

How does the "new ethics" relate to the question of purposiveness in evolution? Whether as a transfer of the maternal impulse or as an independent development, the emergence of concern for unrelated individuals was a supreme event. How did it arise?

It may be seen as the result of a biological "accident," a blind dice-throw of directionless organic shiftings, retained because it helped toward group survival through mutual aid. What we call love, in this view, entered the world as a product of random change in unstable molecules. Like upright posture and the use of tools, it was selected and preserved as useful in the effort to compete and reproduce.

Is there an alternative possibility?

One of the oldest arguments for a purposive divinity is the presence of *design* in nature.* An aspect of design is *organization* in the basic life processes. It is expressed in the chemical and physical laws underlying biological phenomena. Evolution "stems from the laws built into the very fabric of the universe."

---

* Evidence of design as basis for traditional theism was long ago discarded (by Hume and others), but it continues to have meaning with reference to evolution as a directed and creative process. Among other examples is the remarkable way in which the physical universe corresponds to certain mathematical formulae. The fact that "pure reason," apart from experience, can discover features of nature, was characterized by Einstein as the "mystery of mysteries." [14] (His often-quoted comment that "God does not play at dice" may also be relevant.)

Doubts among professionals that the selection formula can alone account for developments at the heart of the evolutionary processes were cited earlier. Complex forms of human behavior without apparent adaptive ("practical") value have been indicated. A biologist writes: "There is a wide range of behavior—and presumably also of evolution—which cannot be reduced to *utilitarian* principles of adaptation of the individual and the survival of the species." [2] The contemporary image of man emphasizes actions *impelled from within*. They are far more than simple products of the needs of adjustment to the environment.[3]

That the beginnings of emotional response to members of the family, clan and tribe, and the impulse to serve them, would favor group life, both animal and human, is clear enough. There is much more, however, than social concern and mutual aid in this sphere of the emotional life. There is a large difference between feeling for family members or for the group as a whole and strong emotional bonds with unrelated persons which are sustaining for a lifetime. Deep attachments of this kind may have power enough to prompt sacrifice of the *group* as well as of the self. There is a difference, too, between benevolence for persons well known and the kind which embraces all creatures everywhere, even those unknown and unloved, human or subhuman.

The chance-plus-selection formula is regarded by evolutionists quoted earlier—and by many more—as far from enough to explain the form and behavior of *some of the lowest organisms in nature.* Is it likely that it can account for an emotional development which reversed the entire trend of natural morality, which gave rise to the most nearly universal of social idealisms and provided the root of the ethics of the world's major religions?

The new emotion was a relatively late event in evolutionary history. If the steadily increasing complexity and variety of living things was purposive, then the new departure was an advance, not a retreat. Here one trend turned against another; the new may have been an outgrowth of the old, but it became, finally, a reaction against it. From some source at work in the depths, there evolved an animal with unprecedented ethical awareness.

Man is motivated far beyond the elementary needs that sustain life. Those who tell us that the process that evolved this goal-seeking creature was itself devoid of goals—that purposiveness came out of a nature empty of purpose— must explain how this could happen. Else we are free to believe that it was there from the beginning.

A number of different trends have been defined in evolution. Philosophers of biology have voiced the right to choose among them with regard to their value by human standards. One of them writes that "man will not . . . deny himself the right to question the wisdom of anything, including the wisdom of his evolutionary direction." Human actions and desires "may be morally right or . . . wrong regardless of whether they assist the evolutionary process . . . in any direction at all." [12]

If, however, there is a trend which is not only basic but in harmony with an ethics on which men can agree, it may be judged worthy of support. The increasing individuality among the members of a species suggests a touchstone for progress. Nothing among the processes of evolution is more basic than the fact of individual variation. Without it there would have been no evolution. If there is an overall movement "shaped by divinity," variation is surely a vital part of it.

This means that the expression of new behavior possibilities is to be encouraged in whatever form they appear so long as they do not conflict with the ethical consensus. In placing high value on the development of personality along with recognition of its worth and dignity, this acceptance of an evolutionary trend is clearly in accord with the morality of Christianity as well as that of other major religions. It is in harmony with a foremost idealism of "morally civilized" societies—freedom of self-expression within the limits of social living. It is in harmony with the fundamental thesis that the emotional root of ethics lies in the deeply grounded response of one individual to the needs of another.

By this token any social change which works toward release of individuality becomes a "good," and the parallel between the two trends provides not only an ethics but one gauge for measuring *progress* in historical movement, itself an important part of the larger question of the overall meaning of human history.

CHAPTER 4

Meaning in History

PEOPLE depressed, insecure or confused about the meaning of their lives may be concerned to some degree with the same question regarding existence in its largest dimensions. They may want to know not only how others like themselves have felt about it, but what professional "thinkers" have been able to make of it.

The question of direction and purpose in evolution was discussed mainly in the context of the animal world. It may be brought into a more vital area when the whole of human experience is explored. What does the historical record show, and what have its interpreters to offer which may sustain morale and give hope? Among other things they have long been concerned with one of the fundamental problems defined in Chapter 1. An outstanding motive to the study of history "is the basic experience of evil and suffering . . . in the last analysis an attempt to understand the meaning of history as the meaning of suffering . . ."

A student of history writes: "The counterpart of the theory of evolution in the biological world is the idea of progress in the historical world . . . there is today a widespread conviction that progress . . . has been and is taking place." Despite this "conviction" it may be noted that the book from which this quotation is taken is titled *The Riddle of History.*[43]

Parallel to the question of directedness in evolution is that of "progress" in the record of human events. A large literature is concerned with the "meaning" of history. That there has been a *search* for its meaning is itself significant; "there would be no search . . . if meaning were manifest in historical events." [38]

The nature of the quest may best be made clear by the kind of questions that have been asked. If there is evidence of directed movement in history comparable to that in evolution, in *what* direction has it been headed? Has the movement been truly progressive, or no more than a series of cycles in which different societies have risen, matured and declined? Nearly everyone with some knowledge of history has read of the "rise and fall" of Rome, or of Assyria, or Persia, or of the Arabs or the Mayas. Such repeated cycles suggest something basic about historical trends. They hint at possible laws.

The questions may also be put in terms of the factors or forces at work. For the religiously minded the force may be Divinity itself, expressed supernaturally in revelation, for example, or more naturally in "Providence." The prominence of great men has suggested that they have been the prime movers in guiding the course of history. Another possibility is that economic processes have been basic to all others.

The simplest introductions may be a doctrine well known to those of Christian faith. Of all readings of the past it has been the most influential in the Western world. "The first and most familiar philosophy of history is the religious one according to which the course of human events shows the hand or the finger of divine providence." [10] The doctrine began, as every Christian knows, with the Hebrew prophets of the Biblical period. "Progress" is here implied in the faith in mankind's advance toward a future *beyond the natural world.*

This kind of progress is not, of course, what the term usually suggests. "What the Gospels proclaim is never future improvements in our earthly condition but the sudden coming of the Kingdom of God . . ." Christian progress is a *spiritual* movement outside of historical change; it is not social, cultural or political. Unlike other views of history, the Christian doctrine is less a philosophy than a theology. The true meaning of the past is here not found in the events of history itself. Textbook history is no more than external or "apparent" history. Behind, or beneath it, "hidden spiritual forces are at work which confer on events a wholly new significance. The real meaning . . . is something entirely different from that which the human actors in the historical drama themselves believe or intend . . ." [13] It is not what historians have studied or what philosophers have tried to explain. It lies invisible to historians; it is under the surface of history as it appears to us.

The essence of the Christian doctrine is that of literal *intervention* into the natural, cause-and-effect flow of events. God has asserted himself "by direct action at certain definite points in time and place." The Incarnation—the supreme intervention—is not only the core of Christian faith but the center of the Christian interpretation of history. This entrance of the supernatural into the natural world was a unique event, certainly the most remarkable that ever happened. Not the least of its extraordinary aspects is the improbable way in which it occurred. "That God should have chosen an obscure Palestinian tribe— not a particularly civilized or attractive tribe either—to be the vehicle of his universal purpose for humanity, is difficult to believe." [14]

An outstanding expression of the Christian view is the *City of God* of St. Augustine: "A vast synthesis which embraces the history of the whole human race and its destinies in time and eternity." Antique though it is, its influence is still active; so much so, in fact, that the author of a recent ten-volume work on history (Toynbee) has been referred to as a "contemporary Augustinian." In Augustine "the foundations of Christian reflection on all major problems were definitely laid . . ." [6]; the *City of God* was one of the hinges of history. "With this book paganism as a philosophy ceased to be, and Christianity as a philosophy began." [22]

It is at outset not something derived *from* the past but a reading *into it* of a theology. It begins and ends in "revealed" truths. The advent of Christ is the peak and turning point of history; faith in his mission is the root of all else. The most familiar tenet of the entire structure is the dictum: "Seek not to understand that you may believe, but believe that you may understand."

Man, in this image of the world, is dependent and in a sense helpless. The outcomes of his destiny are predetermined. The ground of every reality is divine and must therefore in essence be good. Evil cannot be a positive element; "the disorder and confusion of history are only apparent . . . God orders all events in His Providence in a universal harmony which the created mind cannot grasp." [15] There is, of course, much more than history here; the future as well as the past is included. The rise and fall of nations are seen as no more than nodes in the design of a purposive whole, and there lies ahead, all preordained, the Return, the Judgment and the final Kingdom.

This view of history clearly alters the meaning of the word in its usual sense by blurring the difference between the natural and the supernatural. An historian quotes from one of Newman's sermons: "When once the Christ had come . . . nothing remained but to gather in His Saints. No higher Priest could come, no truer doctrine. . . . Earth had had its most solemn events, and seen its most august sight . . ." [16] The rest must be anticlimax, and we mark time, waiting, even though the Second Coming is no longer regarded as close at hand. "All temporal history pales in importance before the supreme issues of eternal salvation or condemnation. Finite life is but a prologue to eternity." [7]

The features of this doctrine are sometimes sharpened by contrasting it with the world image of the classical Greeks. This is of interest in itself at this point, since it illustrates another of the basic views of history.

Much as the Greeks cultivated historical writing "they did not develop any idea corresponding to what we call the direction or development of human history as a whole." As observers of nature they were greatly impressed by its regular repetitions: the movements of the heavens and the cycle of the seasons. The idea of an "eternal recurrence" became prominent in their philosophies. Compared with the world we live in now, in which rapid change is taken for granted, the Greek cosmos was one of repeated rhythms. The historians "were convinced that whatever is to happen will be of the same . . . character as past and present events; they never indulged in the . . . possibilities of the future." [41] For Herodotus events moved, not toward a future goal, but through similar patterns. For Thucydides, human nature being essentially unchanging, the future will differ little from the past; "there is not the least tendency . . . to judge the course of historical events from the viewpoint of a future which is distinct from the past by having an open horizon and an ultimate goal." [42] Although the study of history reached maturity in Thucydides, free of myth, miracles and gods, he recognized "no guiding Providence, no divine plan, no progress." The world of the Greeks was static, finite, complete; they had little sense of history as creative or as an adventure, no idea of growth or development.

The philosophy of history has itself had a history with a long roster of contributors. An inclusive review would be out of place here, but three outstanding efforts may be briefly outlined. They are samples of what such efforts have offered in telling the meaning of the human adventure. They also provide leads toward the final themes and objectives of this book.

Commonly regarded as the founder of modern readings of the past was Giambattista Vico (1668–1744). Far in advance of his time, Vico waited long for appreciation, but finally became a potent influence upon historians as well as those seeking a meaning in the human record.

Although a Catholic Christian with a religious approach to history, Vico's view of the *way* in which divinity works in earthly affairs differed from that of Augustine and is by some regarded as of his greatest originality. The concept of "Providence" is central but he abandons the idea of intervention. God works *in and through the natural processes of historical development*. Providence, though identified with divinity, is expressed not in revelation or direct action but solely through the behavior of men.

Vico's fundamental statement that *society is the work of man* can have little impact for the modern mind compared with its meaning for the world view of the early eighteenth century. It meant that the way things are at any given time is the way they have always been, arising solely out of human impulses and insights. The course of history is determined only by man as he lives, strives and changes, not by controls or "assists" out of a realm above nature. In Vico's century such a proposal was revolutionary. It therefore made its way slowly into the reigning attitude toward human problems and the task of improving man's earthly situation.

Since the course of events is determined by the sum of human motives, this can only mean that Providence achieves its end through those motives. *Man's will, though seemingly free, in reality carries out the divine purpose.* Unknowingly men have accomplished many things they have not intended. *The movements of history, while apparently man-made, are ultimately shaped by Providence.*[63] Whatever Providence designs we may be sure is ultimately good. Whether or not we can understand, "whatever it establishes is order . . . whatever it ordains must be directed to a good always superior to that which men have proposed to themselves." [64]

Vico was impressed by the rise and decline of Roman society and saw in it the formula for a *cyclical* pattern in history. The fall of Rome ended a cycle; a new one began during the Middle Ages and was approaching its end, he believed, in his own century. A cycle has three phases. First is the "age of the gods," in which the monarch is identified with divinity, clearly seen in Egyptian history. The second phase is the "age of heroes," in which certain individuals of superior ability become dominant over the less able; this is seen in feudal aristocracies. It is followed by the "age of men," in which "all men recognize themselves as equal in human nature, and therefore there were established first the popular commonwealth and then the monarchies, both of which are forms of human government."

Vico considered the Middle Ages as a return to barbarism after the fall of Rome, and therefore comparable to the barbarism of the early age of the Greeks. An important difference, however, was the fact that Middle Ages society contained within it the new force of Christianity, which raised it to a level higher than that of the corresponding age of antiquity. His philosophy of history is therefore not truly cyclical; it is rather a *cycle in spiral form. There is advance from one cycle to the next.*

The most important of Vico's contributions with reference to the major themes of this book is the concept of purposiveness ("Providence") expressing itself *in* and *through* concrete historical movements. It would be consistent, for example, with the principle of biological factors as determiners of historical development. His premises permit an intimate fusion of divine agency with natural processes.

One of the major themes of Vico's treatment of history appears with marked emphasis in the next of our "samples," and is often noted as among the prominent features of the work of Georg W. F. Hegel (1770–1831). He proposed that the course of events is determined *by an agency which works within the motivations of men without awareness* on their part of the larger purposes which they serve. They pursue their individual and private goals, yet their strivings may lead far beyond their intentions and "make history." Thus Julius Caesar, to use one of Hegel's examples, was moved in large part by the craving for personal power, but served as means to the movement from one major phase of Roman growth to another. Here again, as with Vico, the directive agency is conceived as working *within* historical processes.

Hegel believed the hidden forces to be at work in all humanity, but most clearly seen in the great men—the "World Historical Individuals"—who have started or helped to form the major movements of events. While such men may have insights into the needs and trends of their times, they are yet means toward goals often beyond their own self-centered aims. "It is not by chance but of the very essence of history that the ultimate outcome of great historical actions is always something which was not intended by men." [39] What impells these men "is not what they are consciously planning but what they *must* will, out of an urge which seems to be blind and yet has a wider perspective than personal interests." Some of them have in fact revealed that they felt driven by urges not of their own choosing and not fully understood. History is filled with unintended consequences and unknowing fulfillments, as if an invisible hand were at work.

It is not, however, so much the individual as the society as a whole that makes the unit of historical study. Every society has certain features which give it a distinctive character or "personality." This is expressed in all its institutions. Foremost among these is religion, and to fully understand a people one must know its religious attitude.

Hegel introduces another major feature of his view of history in his belief that its most vital overall trend is directed toward *freedom*. Ancient societies tended toward despotism; slavery was part of the social structure. Even the "freeman" had few rights compared with the monarch, who alone could be said to be wholly free. In Greece, despite slavery, the freeman had rights of self-expression and some voice in government. In modern Christian Europe the principle of individual liberty is accepted and respected, although it may not be fully carried out. Here the Christian principle of the worth and dignity of the individual has given much to the growth of freedom. In an often quoted summary Hegel states: "The Eastern nations knew only that *one* is free; the Greek and Roman world only that *some* are free; while we know that all men . . . are free." [25]

Freedom for the individual cannot ever, of course, mean entire absence of restraints. It means the disciplined freedom of a person living in a community, and freedom of the community itself from both external and internal domination. Only in a society organized through law is freedom truly possible. The development of the historically important peoples of the world represent stages in a single line of movement: *the evolution of freedom in organized society.*

Hegel here provides a touchstone by which the events of history may be judged as to their meaning for *progress.* The Greek victory over the Persians at Salamis and Marathon, for example, become symbols of the triumph of the spirit of a democratic society over oriental despotism. The high level of individuality among the Greeks was an evidence of the democracy of the city-state in contrast with Asiatic monarchy. But since the freedom of the Greeks was limited to the citizen and rested in part on slavery it was necessary that this society be superceded if mankind was to move beyond it. The culmination Hegel believed he saw in his own time in the Germanic nations of Europe, which had fully accepted the principle of freedom, in large part through the influence of Christianity.

It is not uncommon, in speaking of historical trends and attitudes, to refer to the "spirit" of a period; for example, of Greek inquiry into nature, or of the art of the Renaissance, or of the eighteenth century "Enlightenment." It may refer to an interest or a mood. The term "spirit" is frequent in Hegel's writing, but is it not a metaphor. In his thinking it is *Spirit*, and implies a force or agency. As World Spirit it is basic to all of the movements of history. It is that which underlies the "unintended consequences" of human actions. It is the *indwelling principle which human behavior unknowingly expresses.* It is the root of all advances toward freedom and gives the overall culture of a society its distinctive character. "Spirit" is close to the concept of Providence in Vico's treatment of history. In Hegel's system it is called Reason, and it is equivalent to Divinity.

Others beside Hegel have suggested that deep-lying forces have shaped the course of human history in a way comparable to that of the evolution of life itself. The thought has been expressed in a variety of ways. An historian writes, for example, that "history *does*, to a large extent, go on 'over our heads'; and we *can* often organize the facts of history, as Hegel says we should, in terms of ideas which were not the ideas of the individual agents concerned." [21]

Among the more impressive examples which might illustrate the point are the upheavals which rapidly alter the framework of a society and which have been compared with mutations in organic evolution. Of the French revolution it has been said: "Without question it was not planned by the men who started it: they foresaw neither its early course nor its outcome." [50] The great event was unforeseen "by not only the philosophers and the great monarchs of the day but the men who precipitated it . . ."

Descriptions of the Russian revolution exhibit some notable similarities. Again, much that happened was unplanned and unforeseen. Although long discussed before it began, most of the central figures were surprised by events. It is "something of a marvel that the Russian revolution, the most important political event of modern times, the event which has done more to shape our lives than anything else, should have entered in . . . an unexpected and rudderless way into history." [46] One wonders of how many of the central figures it could have been said, as was said of the Czar himself, that "never at any stage during the revolution's long approach nor at the moment of its outbreak [did] he seem to have understood what was happening."

Again and again the account reflects the uncertainty, bewilderment and improvisations with which the movement began, and the clarity of the fact that *things* were in the saddle. It was a "loose and disjointed" affair, a "confused cracking of the normal surface of life, an experiment." One historian's account repeatedly stresses the lack of awareness on the part of the revolutionaries themselves of the forces at work; "at every moment a dozen alternatives presented themselves, and often it was only by chance that one of these . . . was adopted." [47] The revolution, at the beginning, had "no organization, no leaders . . . it would seem, even no definite purpose." *

No historian would take such statements to mean that an understanding of the past cannot be approached by way of known or knowable factors and processes. The question has yet been raised whether historical movements in their broadest dimensions are *fully* accounted for in the usual cultural, economic and geographical terms.

Biologists have pointed to the absence of grounds for

---

* Professor Hook writes: "Not even the Bolsheviks themselves, who carried out the Revolution and who were committed to a belief in the historical inevitability of proletarian dictatorship, had any inkling that their chance would come so soon." * The Revolution, according to the Bolshevik leaders, would and could occur only in highly industrialized societies. The notion that it might come about in Russia "would have been laughed off as a fantasy"; Lenin himself did not expect it in his lifetime. The only safe rule for the historian, writes one of them (H. A. L. Fisher) is "that he should recognize in the development of human destinies the play of the contingent and the unforeseen." Without unprecedented events, Hook observes, there would be no history.* Hook, S. *The Hero in History*. Boston: Beacon Press, Inc., 1955, p. 185.

assuming that organic evolution in mankind has ceased, nor is it certain that genetic factors may not be related to major differences in the character of races and societies. There have been those who believe we may finally discover that "great cultural movements, such as religious, or other basic historical trends take many of their qualities from the innate physical and temperamental character of the people among whom they originate." [28]

An economist, writing of the vast changes which brought modern commerce and industry out of the simple structures of the Middle Ages, observes that "it was not great events, single adventures, individual ideas, or powerful personalities which brought about the economic revolution. . . . Never was a revolution less well understood, less welcomed, less planned." [26] Some of the factors are now understood, but at the time no one or more persons grasped the massive overall changes nor consciously designed any of them. *Forces, personal and impersonal, were in control and were reshaping the world.* "The new way of life grew inside the old . . . and when . . . strong enough it burst the old structure asunder." Man reacts to trends he does not create, the roots of his actions lie outside of his initiative and often outside of his awareness.*

Views of this kind, which surface often in historical interpretation, are foreshadowed in Vico and Hegel. Despite

---

* Michael Harrington quotes Berdyaev: "The old faith in reason is impotent in the face of the irrational forces of history." Harrington has stressed, as have others, that the industrial revolution was "neither anticipated nor planned." Among other developments, modern urbanization has been "a revolution that took place without conscious revolutionists. . . . Western man has been refashioning reality, and, often without noticing it, himself." In the events of our time we have "lurched into the unprecedented transformation of human life without thinking about it . . . in a sense, this . . . scientific, technological . . . century has happened accidentally." [24]

man's self-awareness, his ability to make choices and to direct his life, the course of history is moved in great part by uncomprehended or uncontrolled forces. The statement that "the laws of biology are the fundamentals of history" suggests that biological and social evolution are related. *What is not fully understood about historical trends may be related to what is far from understood about the processes of biological change.* The creation of culture, which makes man unique, was basically a product of mutation. Men "are the creatures that create culture, because that is the kind of creature they are," and they did not, in any sense, at outset make themselves this kind of creature.[60] Much truth about history may have been summarized long ago by Huntington:

> The general march of progress is directed by deep-seated forces which are only dimly understood. Less powerful forces may alter the general march temporarily. They may produce long periods of stagnation, such as the Dark Ages, or violent crises like our two modern world wars. The effect of such interruptions of the general evolutionary process may last a long time. Nevertheless, they are of secondary importance compared with the basic evolutionary urge which is the supreme fact of history.[27] (A)

The ideas of cycles and that every society is unique were combined, with a new element added, in one of the major modern readings of history—that of Oswald Spengler.

Spengler sought an underlying meaning in the events of the past, a meaning for which all that is actually "visible" is simply an expression. "Does world-history present to the seeing eye certain grand traits, again and again, with sufficient constancy to justify certain conclusions. . . . Is it possible to find in life itself . . . a series of stages which must be traversed . . . in an ordered sequence . . ."[58]

The answer is to be found, he believed, quite beyond the regions where others have looked for it. It is not in historical events themselves. The idea that one event is the *cause* of another is too shallow. This is to look at the surface only. It is the kind of commonsense thinking in which one thing is assumed to cause another solely because it comes *before* the other. This is not only superficial; it is false. "Day is not the cause of night, nor youth of age, nor blossom of fruit."

The key to history lies in a familiar analogy, that of the life course of any living creature: birth, youth, maturity, old age and death; or spring, summer, autumn and winter. The character of every organism, moreover, and the changes through which it passes, depend on the species to which it belongs.

The meaning of history will become clear, according to Spengler, if we apply this idea to the great societies of the past (for example, the Egyptian, Greek, Hindu, Chinese, Arabian) whose separate life courses make up the main sum of the human record. Each one, each culture, in Spengler's terms, is an *organism*, and like any other, its history is simply the expression of its passage from one phase of growth to another. Each culture, moreover, has an individuality of its own and this uniqueness is rooted in its nature.

This clearly means that there can be no world history in any continuous sense. There are many different histories, no one history. The term "culture" covers the entire course of a given society. "Civilization," on the other hand, refers to the declining phase of a society, as Spengler uses the term. Civilization in this sense includes the growth of large cities; increasing pace of living; weakening of traditions; impersonality; "individualism, skepticism, artistic aberration."

It follows that we are all, without any power of choice, shaped and conditioned by the culture into which we are born; "it is not the conscious will of individuals, or even that of whole classes or peoples that decides." None of us is really free; we decide and choose only as we must, as the underlying trends of the culture determine. "When we use the word 'freedom' we shall mean freedom to do, not this or that, but the necessary, or nothing." Like it or not, we move as the organism of which we are a part makes us move, and makes us want to move; "henceforward it will be every man's business to inform himself . . . of what, with the unalterable necessity of destiny and irrespective of personal ideals, hopes or desires, *will happen*." [59]

How seriously is this to be taken? Do other historians agree with Spengler, and is the pessimistic outlook which gave his book its title, *The Decline of the West*, justified? Spengler's view of history has been outlined mainly as an example of one modern view of the meaning of history. The most frequent charge against it has been that it commits a basic error in regarding a society as an organism that must pass through a life cycle like any animal or plant. It is generally agreed that while there are similarities, the differences greatly outweigh them.

More vital to the interests of this study is Spengler's stress on the isolation of cultures. In his treatment each one is a loner, going its own way as a closed system. He fails to acknowledge the ways in which they influence each other. His boundaries are too sharp and too solid. He has been accused of forcing the data to fit his formula.

The idea of cycles of birth, growth, maturity and decline of societies appears in other interpretations of history and seems to support the view that eventual doom is inevitable. This is a conclusion, however, which overlooks the supremely important fact that a society may pass on some of its achievements to those that follow it in time, as well as to its contemporaries. Spengler, in his preoccupation with the individuality of cultures, neglected the vital fact of transmission from one society to another.

Such a failure disregards what is perhaps the simplest of all "philosophies" of history: that the roots of the present lie in the past, and that an enormous part of the content of every civilization is inherited from other times and peoples. For some historians this is the central and only secure finding in the search for meaning.[40] What we know and what we are comes to us in large part from our own past or from foreign sources.

With cultures partly merged and with "export" of creative advances, boundary lines become blurred. Most important, *progress* becomes possible as the total capital of achievement grows and is passed on. That there *has* been progress, in mastery of the environment and in overall grasp of the realities of human existence is affirmed by most historians, at least for specified areas of development. The issue will be resumed.

If any theology may be deduced from history, an historian has suggested, it would be that of a dualism between good and evil forces or "spirits." This may be related to the two great trends in human and animal evolution corresponding to the old and new moralities outlined in the previous chapter. In view of the enormous role of conquest and exploitation in human history, the phenomenon of the natural predator, animal and human, may serve as one symbol of the problem of evil. The essential conflict is often illustrated in the outstanding "conquerors" —the Alexanders, Genghis Khans, Tamerlanes, Napoleons, Hitlers and their kin—on one hand; on the other the great advocates of brotherhood and compassion; the moral philosophers and religious teachers among the ancient

Egyptians, Indians, and Hebrews. It has been seen as a symbol of a basic dualism in history, but also as marking a profound movement from a lower to a higher evolutionary plane, a transition which, if the ethical difference between human and animal means anything, may represent the most significant of all advances in the course of evolution.[A]

Observations by historians and interpreters of history have been cited which suggest that major events and trends have not only been unplanned and unwilled by individuals or groups, but which have seemingly developed without their awareness of the course and meaning of what was happening. *In all three of our sample readings of the meaning of history there is one common factor: the idea that there are forces at work beyond human initiative and full understanding.* Whatever their nature, they are far larger and deeper than any formulated human purpose.

Such statements need not be taken to imply Vico's Providence, or Hegel's World Spirit, or Spengler's notion of culture-organisms. They do suggest, however, that major movements of history have been things that "happened, rather than were made to happen"; that the profiles of events have been shaped by forces working at a level other than that of human plan and choice. In addition to geography, economics and psychology we may need to grant that the processes underlying organic evolution itself have been playing a part.

Those who have derived theologies out of nature and of history—to anticipate the chapter to follow—have seen Divinity internally at work in the human experience as well as in the evolutionary process. God, they suggest, is truly "with us," though in a sense far different from that of traditional religion. *Man, when he makes creative choices, is the medium through which cosmic forces are active. His moral struggles and conflicts are among the points at which these forces converge.* We are not, despite our seeming abandonment and aloneness, separate from deity or "external" to it. *The conflicting trends of historical movement are seen as deep rooted in the core of the sources of life itself.* Good and evil, compassion and cruelty and the war between them, are "one with God, part of his life."

* * *

The existence in nature of over a million and a quarter species of animals and plants clearly shows the value of variation as the key to successful adaptation. Among the lower forms of animal life variation is small in range. It increases with complexity and is at maximum in man, where the range of individual differences is enormous.

Variations, Professor Huxley writes, "became established as an indispensable basis of future progress in the early stage of all the three highest animal phyla . . ." [33] Individuality is here seen as the basis of biological "progress"; as such it is offered as a guide "concerning the direction and methods of human progress." As variation increases the individual himself becomes more important. Nature's tendency toward his sacrifice for the sake of the species is reduced with the more complex forms. "In higher organisms," states Dobzhansky, "every individual is too valuable to the species to be wasted . . ." [19] Professor Simpson recognizes a high degree of individuality as a basic feature of evolution and from it derives the judgment that its development should be one of our goals: "to promote the realization of fulfillment of individual capacities." In the same vein Huxley writes that "anything which permits or promotes open development is right, anything which frustrates development is wrong." [34]

Psychologist A. H. Maslow has proposed, as a solution

to the problem of values, the concept of individual self-realization, or self "actualization." All students agree, he thinks, that this means realizing potentials. It means to become, fully, everything that one *can* become. There are, of course, many secondary goals, but the "single, ultimate value or end of life" is the fulfillment of individuality. Maslow finds evidence for this in the fact that self-fulfilling people, when free to choose, *do* make choices which serve to release potential, thus defining a natural touchstone of value.[44] Among the traits of such people are openness to experience, spontaneity of self-expression, established personal identity and creativeness. They are also democratic and capable of transcending self in their interests. All of these traits are clearly consistent with freedom as a goal of historical development. One of the main functions of related institutions would accordingly be defined as the fostering of individuality.

Such statements by biologists and psychologists offer a touchstone for interpretations of history. They support those who regard increasing freedom as one of the aims of historical movement, if not the chief of its goals. Any change in the human condition which widens the way for individuality may by this standard be taken as one kind of progress. Apart from the positive effect of freedom on the quality of human lives, *it can be only through freedom that whatever purposiveness is inherent in evolution can be fulfilled.*

In this light the main focus for the reading of history will be upon events and trends which have promoted freedom. A recent historian, in a three-volume survey, has traced in clear outlines the course of man's efforts to achieve the great ideal.

For Prof. Herbert Muller freedom means first of all what it doubtless means for most people: "absence of external constraint, or freedom from coercion." A person's abilities and limitations will also be factors. One may be free for an effort, but barred from a goal by lack of knowledge or capacity.

In such a history much emphasis falls on the achievement of personal freedom. Rights must be protected from invasion. The structure of a society determines not only the extent of individual freedom but who is to have it. The history will therefore be largely concerned with progress in extending "rights, opportunities and incentives" to increasing numbers. Muller's statement that "a society becomes . . . freer as it gives more of its members more chance for self-expression or self-realization" is directly in line with what has been said about evolutionary trends. Creativity, as a symbol of self-realization, is "the clearest proof of the reality and the value of human freedom, and . . . a vital factor in its history."

Since the range of choices open to a person is equivalent to his freedom, all gains in technology which extend human resources will contribute to this range. The history of ideas will be a phase of the study of freedom, since they may stimulate or discourage *mental* freedom: "a confidence in man's powers or potentialities, a belief in his dignity or his fitness for freedom." A rigid caste society contrasted with one fully open to change of status in line with abilities would be an example.

Defining freedom as "a state in which a person may decide for himself what is right and good, what to do with his freedom, what kind of self to become," [70] Muller's history shows that among the great movements toward freedom on the European stage were those brought about by the influence of Christianity. Into medieval society the Christian gospel introduced and steadily maintained the concept of human *spiritual equality*, and this despite the enormous differences in the quality of peoples' lives. For all that the Church itself accepted the natural inequalities which kept the great majority at the lower levels of privilege, "there was more democratic feeling in the Middle Ages, and a deeper sense of community, than there had been in the Greco-Roman world, with all its alien peasants and its millions of slaves." [51] Respect for the lowly, in a religion centered upon them from its beginnings, was "a revolutionary reversal of the social values of antiquity."

The Christian doctrine that all men are equal in "spiritual essence" endured through a multitude of violations. Everyone, whatever his deficits, was regarded as having a basic dignity and worth by reason of his divinely implanted soul; "the idea of the sanctity of the person survived all . . . barbarities, to mark another significant difference from the Greco-Roman world." [52] Among the effects of the doctrine was the founding of charity as an institution and the tradition of responsibility for those in need, another contrast with antiquity. In this respect "no other historic church had provided more amply for the needs of simple worshippers."

Certain events have been peaks or turning points in the history of freedom. One of these was the English, or Puritan, revolution, "the prototype of the great political revolutions that have made Western civilization so radically different from all the Eastern civilizations." [53] Its effects reversed the trends in the European monarchies and made a preeminent contribution to the history of Western freedom.

Again one of Hegel's themes is illustrated: the English revolution was confused in its processes, moved by no ideal aims; "no party . . . planned it or guided it to its outcome; instead, one thing led to another, in ways unintended . . ." It finally carried far beyond the purposes of the men who started it. Its chief driving force was religious. The Puritans, in fighting for religious freedom for themselves, became aware that others had a right to it too. They contributed greatly to making the revolution a struggle for freedom for all. Although finally splitting into many sects—itself a token of freedom—they were more deeply at one in a common faith, realizing most fully "the revolutionary implications of the . . . spirit of individualism."

From his survey of Western civilization Professor Muller concludes that growth of freedom has been real and substantial in amount; he sees "unprecedented gains in power, or effective freedom to carry out human purposes, which promoted its extraordinary faith in progress; it has been the most boldly adventurous and continuously creative of the great societies . . . in part because the most committed to a spirit of individualism . . ." [54] The gain has been in the basic liberties of "thought, speech, and press"; in free public education; and finally in freedom of the sexes, most recently in the achievement of equality of suffrage.

For many, progress defined in terms of freedom may doubtless be an acceptable standard, but there are others for which a case has been made. That there have been enormous gains in understanding and mastery of the forces of nature and in material wealth and power is never questioned. On some broader issues of progress Muller feels equally sure: "If all specific gains are disputable, there remains that general advance that man has made, from blind obedience to the totems and taboos of the tribe to conscious, reasoned loyalty to ideals of humanity. All the savagery that persists seems more frightful because it no longer seems inevitable." [48]

In the sphere of human relationships the matter is far less clear. The abolition of slavery is often regarded as the greatest moral advance that mankind has so far achieved.

Any argument in the fields of morality must be painfully embarrassed, on the other hand, by the fact that the greatest atrocity in recorded history—the persecution and extermination of the Jews under Hitler—was an event of our own century.

Yet there is solid ground for hope in the very fact that the human response to such evils has greatly changed, that the horror is itself a measure of increasing awareness and sensibility. The average Roman was rarely concerned about the wretchedness of the impoverished masses of the population, nor was he appalled by the cruelties of the amphitheaters nor revolted by the torture deaths of slaves. Assumedly Romans were emotionally inured in a similar manner at the spectacle of the six thousand gladiators who were crucified following a slave revolt. Social evils are still plentiful; the vital difference is that they are now not only regarded as remediable but are felt by many as deeply distressing. "The barbarism of our times is at least called by that name."

We are here on speculative ground, since the degree of emotional tolerance in an entire society can hardly be measured or even estimated in other than an impressionistic way. We can only make whatever inference seems warranted by such facts as that public executions are no longer witnessed by thousands whose repugnance was assumedly less than their curiosity or enjoyment. In 1757, in Paris, Robert Damiens was publicly executed, following an attempt on the life of Louis XV. The tortures, which were various and included heated forceps and molten lead, lasted four hours and were witnessed by many thousands, who are reported to have cheered when the ordeal was terminated by a dismembering of the still-living body. "The assemblage of people in Paris at this execution was unbelievable. The citizens of near and far provinces, even foreigners, came for the *festival*. The windows, roofs, streets were packed head on head. Most surprising of all was the dreadful impatient curiosity of women who strained for closer views of the torturings." [5] There was much gambling, with wagers laid on the victim's endurance.

Making due allowance for a change, in two centuries, in the perception of the nature of criminal behavior as well as for the effect of habituation to the common spectacle of public punishments, an inference of some security may be made as to moral change as well. That modern atrocities do horrify must have significance.

An investigator of the psychological effects of atrocities (Hiroshima, Auschwitz, Mylai) has described various reactions to the emotional shock of such encounters, such as "psychic numbing" and feelings of guilt.[37] One of the effects of guilt in the case of Mylai was an effort to spread responsibility through a sequence of persons progressively higher in command, finally reaching "the amorphous conglomerate of the American people who, presumably, chose, or at least . . . tolerate" such persons as their representatives. The *felt need* for a distribution of guilt means at least that society no longer accepts infamy at it once did—as an inevitable part of warfare.

Regarding the historical meaning of the Mylai trials a journalist observes that "this is the first time a nation has openly tried members of its own military for brutality or atrocities." [12]

In another approach the issue becames more difficult. One historian suggests that if by progress we mean increase in happiness, the case seems lost at outset. But he also writes: "If we take a long-range view and compare our modern existence, precarious, chaotic, and murderous as it is, with the ignorance, superstition, violence and disease of primitive peoples, we do not come off quite forlorn." [23] If we look above the lowest strata of civilized society we will find that millions have reached mental and moral planes rarely found among primitive men. Progress is beyond question if we regard it as the accumulated heritage of the past; it is richer than ever before, and "we have raised the level and average of knowledge beyond any age in history."

If science has increased control over disease or reduced its pain and malaise the gain should surely be entered on the positive side of the balance. If the heightening of morale that comes with higher valuation of the individual helps to raise the sum total of well-being, this too may be counted against the cost of a more democratic society. With the increase of freedom the frustrations that come from blocked effort and hope are reduced; likewise the defeats when striving itself is denied through lack of opportunity.

Moral progress is most commonly conceded with reference to the recognition of individual rights and the increasingly *conscious* effort to achieve ethical goals. Some have interpreted the enormous recent expenditures of this country in aid of underdeveloped nations as in part a humanitaran movement on a scale *without precedent in human history*.

Freedom itself, however, as we are often reminded, "no more assures contentment than does wisdom, virtue, or holiness." The great Eastern civilizations have made small gains in our kind of progress, but their values have been different. They have sought serenity, detachment, freedom from desire itself, rather than opportunity for the conquest of nature or for a voice in government. They have been "relatively unconcerned about political freedom, failed to develop any tradition of freedom under law of government of and by the people, and made no sustained effort to extend rights . . . and incentives for other modes of self-realization." * [56]

Any references to "happiness" as a touchstone of progress involves the question of its essential conditions. Here again Professor Muller, insightful as a psychologist as well as an interpreter of history, recalls the ancient truth that "the going is the goal," that there may be greater reward in the journey than in the arrival. "Such progress as man has made has not been a measurable advance in the pursuit of happiness, toward any demonstrable prospect of a heaven on earth. It has consisted rather in the very faith in progress, the awareness of finer possibilities and further goals, the sense of freedom and the open road—the happiness of pursuit." [62]

What have psychologists to say about happiness? An increasing number have renounced the view that a complete statement of human motivation can be made in terms of cycles of need and effort to relieve the need, with resulting gratifications. This is the "tension-reduction" formula, usually illustrated in hunger, thirst, sexual desire and the responses to a variety of unpleasant or threatening situations.

Granted that a great deal of behavior is motivated toward sheer removal of an unpleasant sensory or emotional state, a vital dimension of human experience remains. It has been called, among other things, the need of self-realization or self-actualization. When all the elementary appetites and urges are satisfied there may remain, for

* Morris Cohen, with many students of our culture, rejects the identification of technological progress with human well-being, and thinks that "there is probably less happiness in Europe today than in the eighteenth century or even in the nineteenth," [11] one factor being the far greater awareness among all peoples, owing to improved communication, of the enormous inequalities in the distribution of material goods, of freedom and privilege, and thus in the quality of life.

many people (not all), a distinctive kind of frustration, restlessness or incompleteness, as if something within the self were unfulfilled. It may be recognized as a need for *further growth*—vocational, avocational, or creative.

There are modes of personal striving in which *movement in a direction* appears to be all that is sought. There is no terminal phase; no final gratification may ever come. The experience of growth, self-discovery or creativeness becomes an end in itself and yet an activity that never ceases. There are many lives which can be understood only when, as psychologist Maslow says, "a directional tendency must be invoked to make any sense of development through the lifetime." A coming-to-rest never occurs, nor is it desired; gratifications may only intensify interest, and desire is only "for more of the same." Allport agrees that while some motives impell toward mere reduction of tension there are others—the "growth motives"—which mean *sustained* tension directed toward goals which may be distant and even inherently unattainable.

Complete achievement, writes a psychologist, "leaves us hollow and at loose ends. It is only the unfinished tasks that integrate and motivate. Perceiving this fact, Goethe insisted that personal salvation lies always in the striving to achieve, never in mere attainment. . . . That which is not quite fulfilled is best able to hold the attention, guide effort, and maintain unity." [1] Happiness, accordingly, is possible for Faustian man only when he is insatiable.

An American playwright (O'Neill) has expressed the point well: "The people who succeed and do not push on to a greater failure are the spiritual middle classes. . . . The man who pursues the merely attainable should be sentenced to get it. . . . Only through the unattainable does man achieve a hope worth living for . . ." [57] Another dramatist (Williams) agrees that "once you fully apprehend the vacuity of a life without struggle you are equipped with the basic means of salvation." The often-quoted line by Camus is a summary: "The struggle itself toward the heights is enough to fill a man's heart."

Progress, in this psychology, may be measured in terms of one kind of "happiness' and its increase through expanding opportunities for self-fulfillment. It is clearly in line with the view that in one variety of well-being the reward is part of the effort itself rather than the fruit of effort.

It may now be asked how the findings of historians relate to those of the evolutionists. Some of the issues will be considered in the chapter to follow, along with those centering on the questions raised at the beginning of the book. A few leads may be noted here.

Individuality, or natural variation at the human level, includes not only minor departures from custom, habit, the "established order," but more important, departures that are creative and begin new modes of development. If this is the essence of evolution, then the historical fact of increasing freedom has a meaning beyond that of personal experience. Freedom for individuality and creativity becomes the foremost condition for whatever the final outcomes of human potential may be.

One of the trends of modern historical study places main emphasis, not on the discovery of laws, cycles and uniformities, but upon the variety and uniqueness of events and movements. The true meaning of history, in this view, is to be found in the process of change itself, in the unprecedented turn of events. Periods when behavior is relatively fixed, as in the rural margins of civilizations where for centuries there is little or no change in living patterns, mean far less than those of transition or revolution, when the shackles of the old ways are breaking up. Instead of seeking a system or formula, as did Hegel and Spengler, some historians try to learn "appreciation of the subtle shades of individuality, respect for . . . particularity . . . awareness of 'endless formation and transformation' . . . to see in history 'the most exhilarating testimony to the creative vigour, the splendid variety of that human spirit.'" [2]

Against the view of history as a sequence of repeated cycles, one historian believes that it is "a procession of events about which almost the only thing that can be said with certainty is that it moves constantly on and never returns to the same place." [8] There is nothing in history, he finds, to prove that our society faces inevitable decline. There are always sources of fresh drives and developments. One student has emphasized that the *spread* of cultures is approaching a maximum. "Mankind has never before been essentially unitary in culture . . . it is traveling fast that way." [36] Another agrees that society today is *unique not only in technology but in its global character*. All previous civilizations have been geographically limited. Our own encompasses the entire planet, or soon will, and this fact makes it different from all previous ones. It may carry us beyond the cyclical formula altogether and into a phase in which *projections from the past can no longer be made.*[4]

Man's increasing *awareness* of his ability to change things has been seen as one mark of progress. There has been a transition "from the unconscious to the self-conscious" as man sees that he can master his own destiny. E. H. Carr sees increasing consciousness of the potential of a reasoned approach to human problems as "progress." [9]

Biological evolution is rooted in processes which show *both* random changes and guiding agencies. There is evidence of inherent directives somehow related to the extraordinary animal and human capacities glimpsed in Chapter 2, and which to many seem impossibly difficult to understand in terms of planless variations screened by natural selection alone.

The effort to discover overall design in human history has been prompted in part by motives similar to those of students of evolution. The feeling has been expressed that "there is something morally outrageous in the notion that history has no rhyme or reason to it, which impells men to seek for a pattern in the chain of historical events." [65] The cyclical formula still has its adherents, but the fact that the cycles tend toward a spiral is one way of symbolizing the trends of increase in freedom, in control of nature and in moral sensibility. If these are not "laws" they at least suggest purposive movement. Some have conceded that "motives and goals" must be ascribed to entire societies as well as to individuals, and that "in addition to explanations in ordinary causal terms, a historical narrative cannot dispense with . . . purposive . . . explanations." [45]

A few historians, on the other hand, have been led to abandon the search for meaning *within* the course of history and to conclude that it must lie outside of reality as we know it. For Karl Löwith the conclusion is definite: "History as such has no outcome. There never has been and never will be an *immanent* solution to the problem of history . . ." [42] Nicholas Berdyaev rejects on *moral* grounds the idea of earthly progress as a philosophy of history. Man's striving toward Utopian ideals can never excuse the sacrifice of past generations in favor of those of the future. This would mean that "every individual, every epoch of history, are but the means and instruments to this ultimate goal of . . . humanity perfect in that power and happiness which are denied to the present generation." This would leave unresolved "the tragic torments, conflicts, and contradictions of life . . . for all those . . . who have lived and suffered." [3]

Berdyaev would agree with Morris Cohen that "we can not formulate an intelligible account of human history without the use of ethical viewpoints."

Reinhold Niebuhr returns to the traditional view that it can only be through Christian doctrine that the meaning of the past can be found. Christopher Dawson stresses "the mysterious and unpredictable aspect of history" as the main obstacle to all efforts to find laws by which events can be understood. An outstanding example: the unforeseeable influence upon the lives of countless millions of people of the execution of "an obscure Jewish religious leader in the first century of the Roman Empire." [17] On such *improbable* developments, he thinks, only divinity can shed light. It is through religion alone that purpose and coherence can be found in the movements of history.

Those inclined toward this "new supernaturalism" have abandoned the effort to find a meaningful pattern in the natural events of the past. They seek "escape into faith" from the conclusion that history as the historians have written it is without any overall course that will satisfy the need to understand why men have suffered so much, and in ways that appear to be unjust and pointless. Professor Meyerhoff notes a "long and impressive list" of students of history who have returned to the Christian world view after many and various efforts that dispense with religious premises.

The waxing and waning of civilizations has been compared with a series of efforts and failures. The failures have been passing ones, since there has been a quite certain long-term advance. History, like evolution, shows directedness along with apparent chance, as if a *groping intention* were active. "The history of life is comparable to human history in that both involve creation of novelty. Both proceed by groping, trial and error, many false starts, being lost in blind alleys, failures ending in extinction. Both had, however, also their successes, master strokes, and both achieved an overall progress." [20]

The conclusion which many regard as confirmed, however, is that the omnipotent and beneficent deity of traditional religion fails to correspond with the realities. The next question, therefore, concerns the kind of image of deity that is consistent with such findings.

CHAPTER 5

Theologies of Nature

THIS book began with examples of anxiety, depression and lowered morale resulting from experiences which raised basic "existential" questions and led to serious damage to religious faith. None of the subjects had been able to find adequate answers in the current doctrines of the established churches.

The theology most familiar to people of our society has its source in Biblical revelation and in Church tradition. The diety of Aquinas, for example, is the First Cause of the universe and of everything that exists. He is all-knowing and all-powerful. He is also the personality and the purposeful Creator of the Biblical accounts; a Father, Judge and Savior, concerned about man's conduct and his redemption.

Contrasting with this is what is most commonly called "natural" theology. It is founded upon the observed realities of nature and of human life and upon direct inferences from them. It takes the findings of science into account in its conclusions about deity and the relationships between deity and man. Those who seek answers to the basic questions in this way draw "theological conclusions . . . directly from science, claiming that the existence of God can be inferred either from general features of nature, such as design and order, or from specific findings, such as the directedness of evolution . . ." [A] [1]

The history of this approach to a scientific theology extends over several centuries. In modern form it begins with no suppositions taken from tradition or "revelation." It rests solely upon the data of nature. The conclusions thus reached may be fully valid for those who hold them. There are thinkers "who have regarded the arguments for a personal God as convincing, but who do not accept the claims of any special scriptural or historical movement to embody a revelation from him, and hence, rejecting all positive religions . . . have contented themselves with natural theology alone." [13]

The discovery of evolution resulted in marked changes in earlier ideas of the creator by way of its great new light on the *mode* of the creation. After Darwin the divine creative act came to be represented "not as external and once-for-all, but as *within* the process and continuous in time." The distinction between the natural and the supernatural was diminished, with emphasis on the unity of God, man and nature. Some modernists in religion tended to deify the evolutionary process itself. The concept of God as "transcendent" or distinct from the world gave way to that of God as "immanent"—as not only active within evolution but as continuously so throughout its course. The creative process is basic to mutation and sets the guidelines of evolutionary direction.

Much of the groundwork for a theology of nature was laid long ago. The logic is simple: we can learn something about a maker from what he has made. From the fact, for example, that certain physical events follow mathematical laws it may be deduced that something about the creator must correspond to these laws. In ages when geometry seemed to offer the key to the structure and movements of the "world machine" God was sometimes referred to as the "Great Geometer."

If the evolution of life is evidence of a purposive deity, and if much life is periodically destroyed by such natural catastrophies as earthquakes, tornadoes, floods and plagues, it would seem to follow that the power of deity to *secure* his creations has limits. If there has been fundamental change in the "ethical" direction of evolution, as from amorality to morality, it would suggest that a change in orientation has occurred and that deity itself may be evolving. The fact that this change in direction has generated deeply conflicting trends in the emotions and behavior of men implies a corresponding conflict at the core of the creative process.

As to the question whether human experience supports belief in a benevolent God, an historian points out that history is a process of conflict in which the most competent succeed and others fail. It is a struggle where "goodness receives no favors, misfortunes abound and the final test is ability to survive." The total of evidence "suggests either a blind or an impartial fatality." The only theology that human history could support, he suggests, would be that of good and evil forces or "spirits" contending for control.[19]

With these illustrations in preface, some of the conclusions of students of natural theology may be considered.

At outset, the creative *method* is clearly in sharp contrast with the "astronomical instant" (six days) of Christian tradition. The divine purpose required a virtual infinity of time. Granted that duration is a matter involving the

standards of the perceiver, the difference between five billion years (more or less) and the act of a moment is still
an impressive one. Time was apparently a *necessary* condition of the creation, and God, it seems, is a time-limited
creator. As Professor Birch puts it: "People ask, 'Why does
not God make concretely real what is possible for the universe all at once? Why does he wait for billions of years for
the full actualization of himself in the universe? I suggest
that God . . . is a God of creation, and not a magician. At
each stage of the creative process there are limitations on
what can be actualized . . ." [8]

The creative method is clearly *progressive*. The complexity of the higher organisms could be achieved only through
a vast number of intermediate forms. The evolutionary
purpose could be fulfilled only by development; life had
to evolve; it could not be "made."

Evolution includes random as well as directed change. It
is an exploratory kind of goal seeking, a plan with improvisations, like the familiar trial-and-error formula of much
human and animal learning. Organic creation included
blind movements and unforeseeable outcomes. The creator
must be seen as proceeding in part by experiment. He was
limited by an uncertainty factor. The method was based in
part on the principle of sheer probabilities with a near infinite number of "chances."

Much of the animal world lives by exploitation. The
carnivore, human and animal, is a "natural"; the sacrifice
of the exploited species is an essential of nature's economy.
Deeply rooted also is the emotional source of the maternal
care of offspring. In expanded form it is expressed among
unrelated individuals as *caring*, concern or response to the
needs of others. Human ethics rejects the exploitation of
one person by another despite the enormous scale of its
occurrence in nature. The emotional element in this rejection is as natural a product of evolution as the behavior

it rejects. Disharmony in the basic framework must be included among inferences as to the nature of a deity who created both cruelty and compassion.

A theology which recognizes exploitation in the animal world and in a vast amount of human history cannot be harmonized with the God of Biblical revelation and Christian tradition without creating more problems than it solves. Here, again, the existence of suffering, of "evil," is central.

The problem of suffering is of crucial importance because it shows that the God of popular theism does not exist. . . . The theism preached from thousands of pulpits and credited by millions of believers is disproved by Auschwitz and a billion lesser evils. . . . Those who believe in God because their experience of life and the facts of nature prove his existence must have led sheltered lives and closed their hearts to the voice of their brothers' blood.[30, 31]

The logic has been stated many times. If God is omnipotent and permits evil he cannot be beneficent. If he is beneficent and permits evil he cannot be omnipotent. The latter appears preferable, in modern natural theology—a beneficent God limited in powers rather than one all-powerful but evil, or amoral. A limited but *evolving* God, who brought love into the world in revolt against its cruelty seems more consistent with the realities of nature and of human experience than that of one all-potent who yet permits conflict to endure within his creation [(A)]

An image of deity greatly different from that of traditional religion is no novelty in "scientific" theology. It is clearly evident in the writings of some outstanding philosophical thinkers, among them those of A. N. Whitehead and his followers.

Here God is seen as restricted in his power to bring about change in the world. He is responsible for its order, but events occur which he does not determine. Creativity and purpose have their source in him, but he is dependent upon the world for the fulfillment of his purposes. He influences but does not command. He acts upon the world but is also affected by it. He is a "companion" rather than a dictator or judge. He loves the world, understands and sympathizes with man, and suffers with him.[59]

Whitehead's deity is the source of all novelty in evolution. "Apart from God there would be nothing new in the world . . ." [60] God, however, is not himself changeless; he grows in the sense that he is fulfilled as creative events occur which advance the purposes and potentials of the various forms of life. God is responsible for the goals for which we strive, and assumedly desires that these shall be realized. He would be incomplete if his purposes were not achieved. The world is part of his experience, to which he responds, and by which he himself undergoes change. In this sense God evolves with the world; he never reaches "static completion." [61]

Since Whitehead uses the terms "consciousness," "love," "wisdom" and "purpose" with reference to God it is evident that he regards deity as a personalized being. Reality as we know it is the material upon which the divine influence is exerted. Whitehead disposes of the problem of evil by assigning its source outside of God's will.*

---

* Attempts to account for evil have taken a number of forms, among them that in divine view evil is not what it appears to be and has a vital role in the development of personality. Such interpretations tend to be characteristic of religious writers. H. N. Wieman thinks that suffering, "even more than happiness," is an experience "whereby creativity increases the good of life." His view of the benefits of suffering is so comprehensive that he is prompted to say that "not *all* suffering under all conditions is good." Without suffering our lives would lead to "complacent contentment" or to "complacent arrogance." [58]

For the philosopher Royce, man and God suffer together in striving to overcome evil. "You truly are one with God, part of his life. . . . In you God himself suffers . . ." The good is here seen as an essential part of

Among the forerunners of Whitehead in the idea of a limited deity was the American psychologist and philosopher William James. The only God James was able to reconcile with life as he found it is "finite, either in power or in knowledge, or in both . . ." He is supreme within his sphere, but is himself a part of a larger reality. He is "within time," like ourselves; has an environment, is "working out a history." The God of James is a being who calls us "to cooperate in his purposes." He has limits, even enemies, and needs our help. In this scheme evil is an independent element, irrational, alien.[25]

James is clearly among those who believe that we must abandon the notion of an omnipotent deity if we are to be able to have an object of worship. Only a finite God can be worthy of the name, since a God able but not willing to remove evil must lack mercy and compassion, and can hardly be Godlike. †

The Russian philosopher Nicolas Berdyaev formulated a view of deity which remarkably resembles that of Whitehead.[3] Here again God is a limited, striving and evolving entity who suffers with man in his distresses. Berdyaev sees it as a paradox that while God has been traditionally regarded as capable of anger, jealousy, vengeance and love, he has been nonetheless thought of as free of "inner conflict and tragedy." [4]

Berdyaev's God is creative, but his limits are most clearly seen in the concept of *free* forces in the universe. God's

reality; it accrues from the overcoming of evil, and is a greater good than that of a world without evil.[48]

† Nonprofessional thinkers have occasionally expressed similar views. Thomas Mann writes that "God too is subject to development. He too changes and advances . . . to the spiritual and holy; and He can no more do so without the help of the human spirit than the human spirit can do without him." [36] André Gide has observed: "As soon as I had realized that God was not yet but was becoming, and that his becoming depended upon each one of us, a moral sense was restored to me." [21]

work involves conquest of these forces, which did not originate with him, and which are the source of the world's
evil. "The myth of the Fall tells of this powerlessness of
the creator to avert the evil resulting from freedom which
He had not created." [5] God is unable, because of these
"free forces," to foresee the future course of events.

Man is the *medium* of creativeness rather than free to
create in any basic sense. "Man's creative work is the fulfillment of the Creator's secret will."[6] Creativeness expresses itself through imagination, "which springs from the
depths of the unconscious . . ." Man participates in divinity when he is creative.

* * *

The idea of a limited but developing God is consistent
with the moral conflict outlined in Chapter 3. "Evil," as
represented in the predatory behavior in nature, is clearly
not cruelty as we commonly think of it. The animal does
not intend the pain he inflicts; he seeks only to still his
hunger. For man, throughout the hundreds of millennia in
which he lived by hunting, to live at all meant to take life.
He was not cruel but amoral.

With the new morality, with its probable source in the
maternal mammal, the unconscious cruelty of exploitation became aware of itself; aware, that is, of its meaning to
the victim. Gradually, and perhaps at first only in exceptional individuals, something akin to Breasted's "great
transformation" began. Somewhere in the dawn of the new
epoch there emerged feelings of compassion, and with
them the onset of conflict between two elementals, equally
natural.

One kind of "evil," then, is far too general to be an accident of the random factor in evolution. If deity works
within nature, the divine entity is itself in conflict. It must
mean what Whitehead might have called a disharmony in

God's ongoing experience of the world. It means a deity who rejects evil, not in the manner of traditional religion but as part of his own creation. He rejects, as we do, a part of the "self." *

The attitude of man before this new image must differ in important ways from that of traditional religion. It will not be the same toward an all-knowing deity as toward one who through man is striving in the direction of undefined goals. A prayerful posture may seem less than fitting before one whose limited powers have not yet overcome the evils from which protection is asked. In the older formula God is angry or saddened by man's sinfulness. But the "sins" must be charged against their source, not against their victims.

To many, an evolving God limited in powers and creator of a defective world is to be dismissed at once as no God at all. Others may recognize a choice between an infinitely knowing, potent and loving entity who unaccountably permits evils that have for centuries baffled the best minds and a God who made a world badly flawed but who also brought love and compassion into it, and so cannot be wholly devoid himself of something akin to these qualities. † If our rejection of the evils is at source his own re-

* A philosopher wrote, long ago, that "God leads human nature through no other course than that through which his own nature must pass," [49] and Berdyaev observes: "It is impossible to pass judgment on God, for He is the source of all the values by reference to which we judge." [7]

† A correspondent writes: "Sometimes I have felt overwhelmed with indignation and bitterness over the wretchedness in human life and the enormous injustices. Some, without fault of any kind, are so much less fortunate than others. God, I would tell myself, is either indifferent or a bungler.

"Gradually another thought came to me. Great numbers of people must have felt the same revolt and pity, and their feelings are in our nature, as much a reality as the evils. God created them within us, so they cannot be foreign to *his* being. He may not be omnipotent, but he cannot be indifferent or cruel."

jection, and if our failings are his as well, there can be some bond of kinship between us.

A child might find such a choice not hard to make if offered a comparable one: a father full of all the wisdoms and potencies whose love yet seems distant, small and enigmatic; or a father much less perfect and capable, but whose love fails only because he is somehow unable to do more than he has so far done. For the mature adult the most important feature of the choice may relate to his security needs, and certainly a God limited and even in some sense dependent offers less to us in aid. But it means less of fear, and more in stimulus to effort and initiative, and of reliance on self. It can also mean more in feelings of kinship and participation.

* * *

The deity of natural theology has been called a "God of inference" to contrast with that of revealed religion, this to mark the different way in which the knowledge is reached. There is another channel by which such knowledge may be achieved, according to the devotees of a sphere of theology with a long history. It may come directly, through an intimately personal form of *experience*.

In 1945 a professor of philosophy at Princeton wrote an essay in which he said he believed that man's faith in a friendly and purposeful universe was but the wishful thinking of a child unable to face the truth.[52] The truth was "that there is, in the universe outside man, no spirituality, no regard for values, no friend in the sky, no help or comfort for man of any sort." Men, he thought, have been sustaining themselves with "the Great Illusion . . . that the universe is moral and good; that it follows a wise and noble plan, that it is gradually generating some supreme value." If we are ever to *grow up*, we must learn to live with the realities, "stark and bleak" though they may be.

Twelve years later the philosopher published a book which made it clear that he had been greatly impressed by the experiences of men who are most commonly called *mystics,* and who believe that they have been able to make direct contact with a divine being. Professor Stace then stated: "I write as one who . . . believes that mystical experience is in touch with that cosmic Spiritual Presence toward which the great world religions all dimly grope." [53] He was deeply enough impressed to say that even if skeptical students of mysticism should turn out to be right in their judgment that the experience does not *prove* a reality "outside the owner's brain," it is still of high significance; "it still reveals something which is supremely great in human life."

There have been skeptics and believers, with respected explorers in both camps. Stace's own writings may serve as a point of departure, since he is a convert from an agnostic position who must have found weighty evidence in his work in this field. He also writes with clarity and precision.

At outset he distinguishes, as do others, between extroverted and introverted mystics. The one receives his experience from the external world; the world of nature, for example. He sees what we all see, but more, and this more is or may be a definite impression of *unity* or *oneness* underlying or pervading the vast variety of the world.* For some this impression of unity-in-diversity is the central experi-

---

* Stace's description of the core of mystic consciousness as the experience of *unity* sums up much of the writing on the mystical state. William James regards "ineffability" as the most prominent feature, since mystics so often insist that their experience cannot be fully communicated to others.[26]

Professor Kaufmann notes that mystics have by no means been inarticulate and that differences in verbal ability should be considered; emotional states are not always easily expressible in words. "The plea of ineffability . . . is a plea of impotence. . . . The poet who can communicate his experience need not plead that it is indescribable . . . Shakespeare finds words where lesser poets would not." [33]

ence; others go further and identify the unity with deity. A mystic proclaims: "My spirit saw through all things and into all creatures and I recognized God in grass and plants." [54] In the core experience the world becomes "transfigured and unified."

More important, in Stace's view, is introverted mysticism. Here one turns within himself and seeks the essential experience by first clearing his mind, not only of all sense impressions but of all thoughts of every kind. If the clearing is complete, the final result is a state of sheer awareness without content. One is conscious only of *being* conscious, and of nothing else.

Yet this reduced consciousness is *not* an emptiness but a unique and vastly exciting experience of fullness and richness. For Christian mystics this fullness is identified with the Divine Presence and is associated with an emotion of "pure peace, beatitude . . . bliss." For Christians this is the "peace of God"; for Buddhists it is "Nirvana." A mental state has been induced which is somehow at once both empty of content and yet filled with a very definite sense of a *presence*. It is like saying that there is a kind of darkness that is luminous. The experience is well documented in the literature of mysticism of both the Christian and Eastern varieties. There appears to be, beyond question, "something there."

Most students stress the need to distinguish between the experience itself and its interpretation. The latter ranges from the conviction that it is a direct union with God to the view that it is not a religious experience at all. If it is essentially a consciousness of the "unity in diversity of all things," it cannot be regarded as necessarily religious. It is fairly agreed that interpretations are usually made in terms of the religious tradition of the person who has the experience. Different religions give different meanings to the same mystic state. John Dewey has summarized this finding: "History exhibits many types of mystic experience, and each of these types is . . . explained by the concepts that prevail in the culture . . . in which the phenomena occur." [17] Walter Kaufmann thinks that a person will give the mystic experience a religious meaning "only when he stands in a religious tradition." He cites with approval the view that the mystic does not get his theology from the mystic experience but brings his theology to it.[34]

Anton Boisen has reached a different conclusion: that the mystical state is favorable to creative processes and may lead to important advances in thought.[12] The experience of the mystic may be "fertile in new ideas and new insights," and these may be out of harmony with the traditions of his culture. The Hebrew prophets "experienced no mere emotional validation of traditional beliefs . . . but achieved insights of profound significance and lasting value."

Granted that the mind can be emptied of all its usual contents, can the mystic consciousness be understood simply by supposing that a resulting experience of exaltation will or must be interpreted by the mystic in terms of his religious background?

On this view the following comments may be made. (1) It does not apply to the extroverted form of mysticism, which is more common than the introverted. (2) It does not explain why almost anyone should not achieve the experience if merely clearing the mind is enough to set the stage for it. (3) It does not explain the most vital feature of the mystical experience: the strong positive sense of *presence*. The impressive intensity of this experience does not agree with its supposed source in a mental void.[(A)] (4) The mystic experience is possible without a religious background. Those who are "either agnostic or not follow-

ers of any specific religion have reached the mystical consciousness and have still remained outside the pale of any
religious dogma." [72] Mysticism does not require a religious
commitment.

Professor Kaufmann suggests that students of mysticism
have overlooked that "what sets apart the mystic experience is not anything given, but the interpretation . . .
which the person who has the experience accords to it." [34]
The denial that anything is *given* does not seem valid. The
experience has for many persons had an impact great
enough to alter their lives profoundly, and this requires
more than a mental vacuum as stimulus. Nor does such a
vacuum provide the basis for a large literature of interpretation.

If for some the emptiness becomes a Presence, it is not
enough to say that a religious background suffices to explain it. Something extraordinarily impressive happens to
the mystic. As the nonmystic may say that he cannot question the evidence of his senses, so the mystic may say that
he cannot question the reality of the "great awareness." For
him it convinces utterly; his faith in its realness is unshakable. As William James puts it: "Our own more 'rational'
beliefs are based on evidence exactly similar in nature to
that which mystics quote for theirs. Our senses, namely,
have assured us of certain states of fact; but mystical experiences are as direct perceptions of fact for those who
have them as any sensations ever were for us." [27]

James has written of self-observations made under the
influence of nitrous oxide, undergoing experiences which
he felt forced to regard as having a meaning beyond the
natural.* His description, derived from his analysis of the

---

* It was in the context of these studies that James made an often quoted
statement:

One conclusion was forced upon my mind at that time, and my
impression of its truth has ever since remained unshaken. It is that our

literature, agrees well with that of Stace: "The keynote of it is invariably a reconciliation. It is as if the opposites of the world, whose contradictoriness and conflict make all our difficulties . . . were melted into unity." [28] He cites other evidence that the unity experience is "thoroughly characteristic" of the mystical state.

A number of reports have been made of the similarity of certain effects of LSD and other drugs to those of the mystical experience. Impressive parallels and apparent identities are revealed. Both basic forms of the mystical state occur in drug-induced episodes. The experience of unity-in-diversity is reported. The normal feeling of familiar self-hood—the sense of individuality—fades away as it does in "natural" mysticism, while "pure consciousness . . . remains and seems to expand as a vast inner world is encountered."

Within this inner world there is a sense of movement toward contact or merging with "ultimate reality." Vivid impressions of insight or illumination occur. Profound truths about the meaning of existence appear to be within grasp, such insights being beyond logic but felt with complete certainty. The "sense of sacredness" may be prominent, a feeling that what is experienced is *holy*. The mood is often described with such terms as serenity, "blessedness," joy and love. A feature stressed in reports of normal mystical experience is prominent in drug-induced states: the encounter with insights which are convincing despite seeming violations of logic. The subject "may claim to have experienced an empty unity that at the same time contains

---

normal waking consciousness, rational consciousness as we call it, is but one special type of consciousness, whilst all about it, parted from it by the filmiest of screens, there lie potential forms of consciousness entirely different. We may go through life without suspecting their existence; but apply the requisite stimulus, and . . . they are there in all their completeness. . . . No account of the universe in its totality can be final which leaves these other forms . . . disregarded.[28]

all reality. He may write about nonbeing that is more than being." [46]

In summary, for almost every aspect of natural mysticism those undergoing drug-induced states may report closely similar features. One investigator concludes that experimental subjects "experienced phenomena that were apparently indistinguishable from, if not identical with, certain categories defined by the typology of mystical consciousness." * [47]

Do such findings destroy the value of natural mystical states, or the claims of those who regard them as meaningful experiences?

It is important to separate two different effects of drug action. Alcohol, for example, may disturb balance and impair speech, but it may also release social and affectional impulses in an otherwise inhibited person. Psychedelic drugs may cause disorders of perception of form, distance and color, as well as nausea, accelerated pulse and other circulatory disturbance. These effects should be distinguished from those which have led to the therapeutic use of the drugs in emotional problems. For some persons the experience is far more than a pleasant escape or dissipation. It may lead to fresh insights, or to a new attitude toward the self and others. This is by no means automatic; "many subjects report that the subjective sense of work done during the drug session entails as much suffering and exhaustion as would be encountered in several years of living." [46] There may be a stimulus and an inspiration to a change of living pattern in a more positive direction. †

---

* For a critical examination of drug-induced states in relation to mysticism cf. Zaehner, R. C. *Mysticism: Sacred and Profane.* New York: Oxford University Press, 1971, Chap. 2.
† Prof. A. H. Maslow, whose studies of "peak experiences" led him to regard them as the psychological model of religious illuminations, was

While such facts have no direct bearing on the religious meaning of mystical states, they do relate to the dismissal of the total drug experience as a pathological condition. Admittedly the mystical state is limited to a minority, but so are the insights of a scientist, the apprecation of natural beauty by a landscape artist or the raptures of those who respond strongly to classical music. † Both the psychedelic and natural modes have led to better organization of personality, lifts in morale and greater serenity.

Prof. G. F. Thomas thinks that many "if not all, of the great religious leaders have had experiences which were in some degree mystical." [56] He finds marked similarity in the mystical states in different religions and is impressed, as are many others, by its profound effects upon the personality. The mystic often "acts with a poise and serenity lacking in most of us." (A)

The language of the mystics arouses a responsive feeling in most people, Thomas believes. He interprets this to mean that there is no real separation of the mystic state from experiences familiar to some degree to many persons. He regards it as the exceptional development of a *normal* form of religious emotion.

A different view is that of Rudolph Otto, who has written extensively of the mystical experience in both its Eastern and Western varieties.[44] He regards it as a primary mental state which cannot be further analyzed. The capac-

---

among those who viewed psychedelic drugs as a possible means of inducing the experience in people low in capacity for it as well as for research into these states.[37]

† It has been established, states a sociologist (Max Weber), "that men who are *differently qualified* in a religious way stand at the beginning of the history of religion." "The sacred values . . . the ecstatic and visionary capacities . . . could not be attained by everyone." He compares those who lack them with people who are "unmusical," assumedly in basic abilities.[57]

ity for it cannot be acquired; it can only be awakened. The
unique gift he regards as the true source of the world's religions. The mystic state is deeply moving and he stresses
the limits of language in any attempt to convey its quality.
It is "a strange and mighty propulsion toward an ideal
known only to religion . . ." His book *The Idea of the Holy*
is eloquent in description of the experience.[45]

The number of persons with capacity for it is unknown.
A contemporary mystic (Sri Aurobindo) has proposed that
it represents a new development in mental evolution. "If
we could accept this," Stace suggests, "we would expect
that the small minority of men who have now reached the
mystical stage will gradually . . . become a majority . . ." [55]

That continuing mutation in human evolution is a possibility is conceded by respected biologists ("Man has not
only evolved, he is evolving"). Man differs from the lower
animals mainly in mentality, and it is assumed that new
mutations will occur at this level. Suggestions similar to
that of Aurobindo have been made with reference to other
"psychic" phenomena (e.g., clairvoyance, psychokinesis,
etc.).

Among the individual religious experiences of mankind
those of the Hebrew prophets of the Biblical period were
of far greater influence than the "illuminations" of the
mystics. Professor Kaufmann has suggested that the crucial events in the lives of these men, while somewhat like
mystical states, were a different phenomenon. He suggests that they be termed "inspired," since to call them
"revealed" would be to go beyond the facts. They were
experiences of contact with a source of great power. Their
role in the origin of one of the major religions of the world
is well known.[35]

The word "inspiration" suggests something that *happens* to a person rather than what he brings about by in-

tention. A description which has become a classic is that of Friedrich Nietzsche. Those who have known it, he thinks, "could hardly reject . . . the idea that one is merely incarnation, merely mouthpiece, merely a medium of overpowering forces . . . one accepts, one does not ask who gives . . . a thought flashes up, with necessity . . . I never had any choice. . . . Everything happens involuntarily in the highest degree but as in a gale of a feeling of freedom, of absolution, of power, of divinity." [43]

In some religious leaders such experiences were only occasional; in others, among them the Hebrew prophets, they were frequent and prominent. James notes "distinct professions of being under the direction of a foreign power, and serving as its mouthpiece." He quotes from an analysis of the experience of the prophets:

One after another, the same features are reproduced in the prophetic books. The process is always extremely different from what it would be if the prophet arrived at his insight into spiritual things by the tentative efforts of his own genius. There is something sharp and sudden about it. He can lay his finger, so to speak, on the moment when it came. And it always comes in the form of an overpowering force from without, against which he struggles, but in vain. . . . It is not, however, only at the beginning of his career that the prophet passes through a crisis which is clearly not self-caused. Scattered all through the prophetic writings are expressions which speak of some strong and irresistible impulse coming down upon the prophet, determining his attitude to the events of his time, constraining his utterance, making his words the vehicle of a higher meaning than their own.[29]

* * *

What is this to mean to us and how does it fit into the background of our discussion at this point?

Purposiveness in evolution centers upon the mutations

which advance into higher forms of life. The human parallel is the original departure in the realm of thought: an insight without precedent, the perception of possibility, a flight of imagination. If deity works, above all else, in the creative process, then man's closest approach to life's most personal as well as directional meaning must lie in individuality of the kind that leads to new trends.

Our experience of *choice* ranges from those in which we feel we have initiative to those in which mental events seem to thrust upon us and to various degrees dominate. Among the many examples are some of the creative products of genius, the insights that appear to come from subconscious levels, the mystical states and the inspirations of nonmystical religious innovators. Here the individual is more like a witness or medium; he is "subject" to the event; his initiative is small or absent.

If the roots of evolutionary change are still active it must be among experiences of this kind that they are manifested. If there is truth in the view that deity is active *within* creative behavior, it must be here, if anywhere, that the action is made known to us. In this light biology and theology become merged, and the advent of the Hebrew teachers, for example, may be said to represent a great creative movement from the "old" ethics to the new. Rivaled only by the growth of man's control of nature, it meant the growth of his control of himself. It was the conquest of the ethics of force by that of love and compassion.

The God of Christian tradition gave freedom of choice to man, who then became responsible for much of the world's evil and so burdened with guilt and a need of atonement and redemption. This doctrine has been replaced, in some of the "natural" theologies, with the view that man has not only been entirely formed by evolutionary processes which he is far from fully understanding, but that he continues to be the medium through which deity is fulfilling some ultimate purpose, however unclearly defined.

With this conclusion we are confronted with a fundamental question: What does man's experience of individuality and of freedom mean if his role is that of a medium of evolutionary design? In what sense, if any, can he be said to be *free?*

Some of the limits on freedom are easy to see. Those set by the social milieu are always most heavily weighted by psychologists and sociologists. All of us are molded, in the home, the school and the countless influences of community life into a very large part of what we become. The century, the nation, the social class and the family into which we are born are the major shaping elements that determine the choices offered us.

Others are internal. A person's life may be markedly affected by his mental limitations; careers may be closed if abilities are poor; personal deficits may narrow mating choices and friendships. The ability to enjoy life may be impaired by a depressed, anxious or otherwise neurotic temperament. Choices may be narrowed by physical disease, low vitality or a congenital deformity.

Man is commonly said to be most nearly free when his thoughts, desires and impulses are most fully released from the pressures of habit and the need to conform. He is free when he can be most truly and deeply "himself"; when he can allow all feelings to emerge into awareness and when he can think in his own distinctive style; when in brief, he can most fully give way to his "individuality."

But if it is at just these times, when the pressures toward conformity are at minimum, that he is most under the influence of those deep-lying forces which make the grounds of his individuality, in what sense can he be said to be "free?" If these are the moments when he *feels* most free, is this feeling in reality an illusion? Is he, despite the experience of release, merely subject now to the root factors of his uniqueness?

To be free may mean release from internal pressures and demands as well as from external ones. A person may desire escape from the craving of the tobacco habit or for alcohol or drugs. He may be burdened with an anxiety, or be struggling with a neurotic obsession, or feel emotionally bound in a sexual attachment. In many cases a person may wish for release from such a demand within himself. One may want something and not *want* to want it. A middle-aged housewife prayed nightly for strength to overcome her neurotic eating habits. A young woman in the throes of a love affair said, "I hate caring so much; he'll have me completely in his power." Such internal pressures may force a person "against his will" to behave in certain ways.

Does the *absence* of such pressures mean "freedom," in any fundamental sense? The above examples represent conflicts of one desire with another. An impulse may conflict with an ethical standard or with one's self-esteem. A choice may, on the other hand, present options which are not in conflict. They may be incompatible only in the sense that they cannot both be satisfied, as in a choice between two attractive careers. Freedom of choice then means freedom to choose on the basis of the stronger interest. One finds himself responding to one option to a greater degree than to another. His choice may then be made on this basis, but he may also find that *at no point in his past was there any decision regarding the strength of interest itself.*

A great variety of choices are of this kind. The background may reveal factors which appear to show how interest was first developed. Or no external influence may be discoverable, and it will be clear that from the beginning there was *inclination* to respond, as is often and most clearly seen in gifted people, especially in the arts and sciences.

The main point is that regardless of background, the choice has been *determined*, either by external factors, by spontaneous feeling or by a combination of both. One may choose as he wishes, but without choice in the character and direction of the wishes themselves.

One student of the issue of "mental" freedom summed it up at the most concrete and elementary level:

I *am* free to make choices on the basis of my strongest urges, desires and purposes, and under the guidance of my beliefs, my acquired knowledge and accumulated experience. I have *not* had freedom of choice with regard to the strength of my various urges, desires and purposes, nor with regard to the strength of my beliefs or the character and amount of my knowledge and experience. I may act according to my "character" or my basic dispositions and temperament, but I did not choose these, nor did I ever choose them, any more than I had a choice of my parents, my physique, or the circumstances under which I grew up, or the influences that molded me into what I am.

After centuries of debate, no valid case has yet been made against the premise, basic to psychology as to other sciences, that human behavior, as all else in nature, is fully determined, and that the *experience* of freedom is an illusion. For concise clarity it is possible that Spinoza's statement has never been much improved: "Men believe themselves to be free, simply because they are conscious of their actions, and unconscious of the causes whereby those actions are determined . . ." They are "conscious of their volitions and desires, and never even dream, in their ignorance, of the causes which have disposed them so to wish and desire." There is no "absolute or free will"; the mind "is determined to wish this or that by a cause, which has also been determined by another cause, and this last by another cause, and so on to infinity." [51] What we call "will" is essentially desire, and our decisions, however they may appear to us, are finally reducible to desire.

Persons quite willing to regard themselves as subject to thoughts, impulses and moods that are unwanted or unaccountable, may find themselves less able to admit that they do not initiate, control or desire to control urges which may yet be strongly impelling. Neurotics have more opportunity to experience the compulsiveness of unaccountable emotional states and impulses.

People differ in personal response to the idea that we do not, in the final analysis, have freedom of choice. The usual reaction tends to be one of resistance. For some, to think of oneself as subject to motives of unknown or "unconscious" sources may seem oppressive and even degrading. Others may find it acceptable from a different point of view. To feel that one's individuality or one's highest goals and values are expressions of forces deep in a realm continuous with creative evolution, or that one is an agent or medium for such processes, may be experienced as stimulating and even exalting. Examples are often seen in those who have felt impelled by a "mission," or that they were "chosen" to achieve or to serve in some way.

A successful business executive with a well-developed avocational interest in "creative writing" expressed himself in this context as follows: "I don't know where this comes from. No one in my family feels as I do about wanting to do something original in literature. It started during my 'teen years' and became increasingly strong. I believe that if for some reason I had to abandon the hope of some day succeeding I would feel utterly lost and empty. Unless I can be a creative person life would be hardly worth living.

The only time I feel deeply happy is when I think I am making progress."

This man was much impressed with the life of Paul Gaugin, whom he regarded, like himself, as a "victim" of the compulsive urge toward creative achievement in art. He also quoted Pablo Picasso: "Painting is stronger than I am. It makes me do what it wants." "A real artist," writes one of Thomas Mann's characters (*Tonio Kröger*), "is not one who has taken up art as his profession, but a man predestined and foredoomed to it . . . ."

It has been proposed by certain "existential" writers that since, as they believe, neither evolution nor human history has a clearly evident meaning, it is open to man to give himself a meaning—to "make his own meaning." He must accept the challenge as an opportunity to decide what he wants to be and what kind of world he would have.

This is on the surface reasonable enough, but if our premise is valid it may also be said that whatever this decision, it will be at root no more free than any other. It will have its determinants, known or unknown, and these will lie not only in the background of the individual life, but somewhere along with the "internal factors of evolution," among the processes that make each person a literally unique creation.

If we are free to do what seems best to us, then what will seem best will appear so because of the factors and forces that have formed us, and which no one of us has ever chosen for himself. If the choice that is made seems reasonable it will be because man is in part a reasonable creature, made so by his processes that evolved him. If he is impelled to make his choices in certain directions because of the "needs of his nature," those needs are as much a product of "depth biology" as are his powers as an intelligent animal.

Even at those times, therefore, when it can be said that a person's actions are to a high degree an expression of individuality, he is not in any basic sense a spontaneous agent, or "abandoned to freedom." Whatever moves he makes will be to some degree guided by factors at the origins of his uniqueness. Whatever he will want to do in the decisions most important to him will be an expression of his whole and deepest nature.[A]

If, finally, a creative entity is actively at work in the evolutionary process, it would seem permitted to believe that it touches us most intimately at times when we are deciding what we most want to become. *It may be at moments when we most acutely feel our freedom that we are most closely in contact with that entity.* What a person thinks, feels or does when he becomes free to do what he experiences as most nearly of "ultimate concern" to him will be his closest contact with the core of *his* distinctive purpose in being. So far as the genetics of creation are expressed in him this choice will be an answer to the question: What am I for?

From this it would follow that *everyone is a medium, to some degree, of purposes larger than he knows.* The philosopher Hegel believed that a cosmic goal is in fulfillment through the actions of individuals who all the while regard themselves as serving their own ends. Others have more recently touched upon the same theme: "Writers of many different schools of thought have concurred in remarking that the actions of individual human beings often have results which were not intended or desired by the actors or indeed by any other individual." [16] That there is a "hidden hand" at work in human affairs is a concept with a long history quite apart from its traditional meaning. An historian observes: "There is something in the nature of historical events which twists the course of history in a direction that no man ever intended." [15] A student of the modern revolution in technology, impressed with its effect in molding the lives of countless millions, observes that it came into being "without their really grasping what . . . happened to them and independently of any individual's will." [62] A novelist-philosopher (Tolstoy) wrote: "Man lives consciously for himself but is an unconscious instrument in the attainment of the historic, universal aims of humanity."

* * *

A philosophical biologist has pointed out that a universe in which the end was predesigned or "settled" from the beginning would not allow for any truly creative event. Another writes: "Evolution is a creative process. It could never be called that if it were simply the unfolding of completely preordained pathways. There is no creation in a completely deterministic system." [9]

How can the concept of a creative cosmos be reconciled with that of *determinism* in human life?

The sources of creative change (mutation) are far from fully known. They are expressed in the evolutionary process and in certain human choices. The idea of a limited God is consistent with the view that he is a directive agency in evolution but that his control is not complete. He cannot foresee all outcomes.

Man himself is "free" to respond to the forces of change, but they express only *through* him. He experiences the creative movements, but is not himself literally creative. He experiences the options but does not make them. He feels the promptings but is not their source. If deity is limited, man is surely more so, if "deity" is to have any meaning. A universe which contains chance as well as directives can only mean that there are forces at work which neither God nor man can fully control.

Whitehead and others have stressed that the power of

deity is "persuasive" rather than coercive. Birch, for example, states: "The doctrine of the divine agency as a persuasive and not a coercive agency is one of the greatest intellectual discoveries in the history of religion." [10] It may be inferred that God *can* only "persuade" or influence, or set going the forces within his power.*

It may be the ultimate paradox that man, overwhelmed at the mystery of his own genesis out of inorganic nature, should at times talk as if he can "make himself" as he wishes.

* * *

Individuality, or variation, is a central movement of the life process. Without it there would have been no evolution. It is the outstanding evidence of purposiveness in the history of organisms. Evolution has ceased in certain animal forms and individuality is small in range among the lower ones. It is greatest by far in man. High degrees of individuality are among the sources of major historical trends. The advent of such figures as the Buddha, Jesus, Mohammed, Newton, Darwin and Marx are among those often cited.

Whole peoples as well as persons may exhibit the trait. Certain societies are described as artistic, commercial, warlike or animated by an adventurous spirit. Students of behavior impressed with the great importance of environment in molding habits and character have assumed that all or most "people differences" must be social products. Yet if individuals can differ biologically, so can groups. A biologist writes: "Race differences are compounded of the same ingredients as differences among individuals which

---

* Taking persuasion to imply incomplete power is in line with references to nonrational and *refractory* elements of divinity (Brightman). Berdyaev has written of aspects of divinity which represent an irrational "dark side." In the "primal depths" there is "tragic conflict." Traditional doctrine has always envisaged divinity as free of all disharmony and contradiction, refusing to acknowledge the evidence of "irrational forces of obscure origin." [4]

compose a race. . . . If individuals . . . vary in some character . . . it is quite unlikely that the population[s] . . . will be exactly the same." [18]

Once culture traits are established they will tend, of course, to be transmitted socially, but biological factors must help to account for the fact that a culture may be "peculiar" from its beginning. "Since creativity in the individual . . . involves unconscious processes, we may assume that equivalent factors have been among those operative throughout man's history." [22]

The Hebrews of the Biblical period have been cited as having made the most important advance in the ethical development of Western civilization. It has been suggested that they were biologically "biased" toward the new morality; they were, like the classical Greeks, "an extraordinary human phenomenon." The advent of the prophets, culminating in Christ, made them unique. "The birth of Christianity is one of the central dramas of human history. The enormous influence of Jesus and a handful of humble Galilean country folk exercised upon subsequent generations staggers the imagination. . . . The actions, thoughts and feelings of these few men profoundly affected the acts and thoughts and feelings of hundreds of millions." [40]

An historian notes, as have others, that the teachings of Jesus were "no more than an emphatic assertion of ideas already familiar in the Judaism of his day." Jesus "was essentially another Hebrew prophet," although he "deepened and expanded those teachings of the great Old Testament prophets which had proved most challenging and spiritually fertile." [13] He gave expression to a larger conception of neighborly love as a religious duty: "My neighbor is any human being in need, whether he belongs to my race or to another." [14]

A scholar in Old Testament literature has marked the originality of the prophetic movement as a whole. The unique advance was made by a series of exceptional men. The moral tradition they established was the work of centuries; some of its roots may have been lost in prehistory.*

Unlike the religious devotees of other cultures, the prophets were little concerned with ritual; they centered their labors on morality and social justice. In the Law of Moses "the unique worth of man as such is proclaimed . . . for the first time in human history." In a famous Babylonian code a slave was a chattel, less than human; his treatment and especially his punishments differed from those of aristocrats and commoners. In the law of Moses, "the slave is first of all a human being and has to be treated as such." The great modern idealisms of equality and fraternity are rooted in the Old Testament in the doctrine that every man has dignity by reason of the very source of his creation. Everyman is a self, never merely an *object*. Violation of the meaning of brotherhood is therefore central among the sins; "no other sacred scripture contains books that speak out against social injustice as eloquently, unequivocally, and sensitively as the books of Moses and some of the prophets." † [32] This sensitivity distinguishes the Old Testament "quite radically" from the New, from the Koran and from the sacred books of India.

* Walter Kaufmann concedes the Egyptian influence but maintains the uniqueness of the Hebrews in their *response* to it, which seems valid if the intensity and richness of a reaction to experience may itself confer originality.

† "The characteristic genius of the Jew," writes Edmund Wilson, "has been especially a moral genius. The sacred books of the people of Israel have served as a basis for the religions of three continents; and even in the case of those great men among the Jews who do not occupy themselves with religion proper, it is usually a grasp of moral ideas which has given them their peculiar force." [63]

The evolution of the Hebrew deity from a militant God to one of benevolence and justice—"from a religion of fear into one of love"—was the work of individuals of exceptional awareness of ethical values. References to "the passion of the prophets" stress the *emotional* foundation of their responsiveness to those values. "Isaiah and Amos began, in a military age, the exaltation of those virtues of . . . gentleness, of cooperation and friendliness, which Jesus was to make a vital element in his creed. They were the first to undertake the heavy task of reforming the God of Hosts into a God of Love . . ." [20]

If there were individuals in every human society during and after the first millennium B.C. who experienced in some degree the thoughts and feelings of the Hebrew moralists (as there certainly were, according to Breasted), there must have been many before that period. It appears that what occurred during Old Testament times was an extraordinary *intensification* of moral awareness, with eloquent expression, in one group of people, but a trend never confined entirely to any one group.*

In summary, the Hebrews were truly a "chosen" people,

---

* The individual whose originality lies in this kind of emotional sensitivity is illustrated in Edith Hamilton's observations on the classical Greek playwright Euripides. This dramatist was "the poet of the world's grief." He *felt*, as no other writer of his time, she states, "the pitifulness of human life, as of children suffering helplessly what they . . . cannot understand." His sense of the value of each individual was one in which the world he lived in was almost lacking. "He alone of all the classic world so felt. It is an amazing phenomenon. Out of the pages written more than twenty-three hundred years ago sound the two notes which we feel are the dominants in our world today, sympathy with suffering and the conviction of the worth of everyone alive." (A) [23]

Three hundred years earlier, writes Hamilton, there was another "completely modern mind who felt, as no one has ever felt more, the pitifulness of human life and the intolerable wrong of human injustice, and whose eyes were keen to pierce beneath fair surfaces—the greatest prophet of Israel, Isaiah."

but in the biological sense that they were the medium through which the trend of the new evolution was more strongly expressed than in any other known in history, and beyond question the most influential. On the premises of a natural theology the "revelation" came to them, not as a voice from the infinite, but through the emotional experiences of a series of individuals gifted beyond the ordinary with compassion for the victims of the natural inequalities of mankind and of human aggression.

They represent, like the Greeks, though in an entirely different sphere of achievement, one of the great surges of the advance of the evolutionary process. For those who value the quality of human relationships above that of the material fruits of science, the Hebrew contribution to civilization will be seen as more precious than that of the Greeks. Such a conclusion may be acceptable to all those who believe that our salvation today, as a society, is more dependent upon tolerance and goodwill than upon progress in technics.

CHAPTER 6

Psychological Solutions

THE views of some who have found a basis for faith in the evidence of design and directedness in evolution and of meaningful movement in history have been outlined. An image of deity more realistic than that of tradition has been considered.

Compared with the solid certainties of orthodox faiths, such findings may seem thin in substance. For those content with established doctrine, they must seem little more than speculations of small worth and unthinkable as alternatives. For the increasing numbers who have for various reasons found the "institutional answers" no longer convincing, these offerings may be of some value, it is hoped.

There remains a further resource, and one which should perhaps be the most fruitful of all, and to which much of the discussion might seem to point—namely, human psychology. What does it have to offer? A writer on the "crisis" in psychiatry and religion observes that many psychologists "are now turning their research interests toward problems which have long been of concern to religion and church leaders." [60] The interest itself is certainly relevant to the times. Another writes:

at just this juncture of the world's history literate people are growing more and more concerned with the relation between psychology and religion . . . while the majority subscribe to the tenets of an historical faith they find that they hold the faith with many mental reservations. Why, they wonder, do doubts increasingly haunt them? . . . while they still "feel" religious, the regulative principles for their conduct are coming less and less from their religious belief and more and more from psychology, psychiatry, and mental hygiene.[2]

What have professionals to offer on the "psychology of religion?" They are agreed at outset that there is no inborn religious response to the world, nor is there an emotion peculiar to religious experience. There is no unique religious emotion. What is felt in a religious context are simply the familiar emotions in a different setting. Religious love, for example, "is only man's natural emotion of love directed to a religious object; religious fear is . . . ordinary fear . . . so far as the notion of divine retribution may arouse it." [42]

Religious psychology covers a wide range of views. For one student the idea of God is simply a projection of the human need to believe that there is one. "Thus the great religions of the world are not theology but psychology . . . God . . . is the image of man, projected, enlarged, upon the empty canvas of the universe." [78] Freud regarded the idea of God as no more than an expression of the unconscious need of a father figure. It is an exalted image rooted in the child's regard for the father as an omnipotent being. Others emphasize man's tendency to see supernatural figures behind the phenomena of nature. Eventually he identifies such beings with the highest of his social and ethical values.

Prefaces to a psychology of religion often include examples of the ways in which it reflects the culture of which it is a part, and how the image of deity changes with the evolution of a people. For an agricultural society the important gods are those in control of fertility, growth and the seasons. For a warlike culture the deities will be "gods of battles."

Most psychologists agree that religions are products of human evolution, that they have grown and changed like other elements of society. They are ways of thinking designed to give meaning to life, and tend to center on belief in personalized beings who become linked with feelings of awe and reverance.[41] Religions are never finished products so long as societies continue to develop. Our own are not likely to remain fixed in character, however slowly they appear to alter.

The religious attitude is highly varied. It may be a doubt-free and unthinking acceptance of traditional doctrine, engrained from childhood by inheritance from parents, church or both. It may be the product of much thought and examination, with transfer from one set of doctrines to another. It may result from sudden and highly emotional conversion, or from what is experienced as a direct contact with divinity, as in mysticism. It may be based on analysis of the pros and cons and a reasoned conclusion from a balancing of evidence. For a few it may be a commitment knowingly uncertain but with a belief that life is more productive if we assume that it has meaning. A college student states: "I think the best working principle is to live as if we are entirely alone and that everything depends on our own efforts. Then, if there really is more to it than we know then we'll still be ahead. If there isn't, we won't have wasted any time banking on outside help."

Another student reports:

My reasoning about God and immortality is based on simple ethics, not on science or the Bible. There is so much inequality in peoples' lives that is absolutely no fault of their own. To me this is the most impressive thing about human life, that some people have so much more of everything than others.

To me the only believable God is *just*, and this has got to mean an afterlife and *justification*. Nothing else can give any meaning to religion. Without ultimate justice I would reject everything completely. Life would be an unspeakable crime. I would want no part of such a universe and I would be quite willing to leave it.

A variety of "natural" theologies are worked out on an individual basis. A business executive, age forty-two, expressed himself as follows concerning an important turning point in his personal philosophy:

For a long time I had periods of depression and moods of bitterness over the way my life has been. I have failed to reach my goals because of setbacks and mistakes I've made owing either to mental limitations or to defects of personality I did not realize until it was too late. I've had the thought that I've been the same kind of loser as people with chronic diseases or congenital deformities, only my misfortunes have been psychological instead of physical.

I finally worked out an idea that changed my attitude and reduced my depressions. If there is a God who is really benevolent and loving, then the miseries of life will somehow be righted. But if this is not true and life is really what it seems to be, then my position is that instead of feeling that *I've* been a failure it is life itself that is a failure. The unfairness would be so great that I just can't *take it personally any more*. I think of the poor wretches far worse off than I've ever been. In spite of my depressions I've been better off than vast numbers of others, so what right have I to ask more? I used to ask *why me*? Now I ask why *them*, or why *us*? I still feel low at times but I don't have the personal bitterness I had in earlier years. It's a matter of seeing things on a larger scale. I can feel almost as distressed for others as for myself.*

Gordon Allport has marked the variety of motives that prompt religious behavior, both from one person to another and in the same person at different times, according to his needs. "When we need affection, God is love; knowledge, He is omniscient; consolation, He granteth peace. . . . When we have sinned, He is the Redeemer . . ." [3]

Most psychologists see social influence as the major

* The following statement by a member of one of the writer's therapy groups is illustrative, not of a theology but of a rationale with comparable support for morale. He headed it "A Philosophy for Failure."

The most sustaining ideas that came out of our discussions developed after I left the group, but they resulted from thoughts and feelings I had during the meetings.

Much of my life has been blighted by the simple fact that my ambitions have always been greater than my capacities. Always in the background of my mind was the really strong drive to be great in some way. I've had many fantasies of being a genius as a writer or a scientist. At heart it has been a craving to excel.

Well, I have failed pretty completely. I'm definitely a mediocre person, and now I know I'm too old to ever be anything else. There have been times when this basic frustration has made me feel quite bitter. It's as if I were as much a "handicapped" person as someone chronically ill, or born blind or crippled.

It was during the group work that the idea dawned on me that there is *fellowship* in man's existence as well as achievement. There is a basic brotherhood among us as well as status and comparisons and superiority. Perhaps a deep friendship can mean as much as being outstanding in some way. If you really love someone it doesn't matter whether they are superior or not. I know a woman who loves her imbecile child more than anything else in life.

But more important even than this is something I believe in absolutely, that the truth about our brotherhood is deeper and greater than the truth about our differences in ability. We are all creatures of inheritance and our circumstances. Our spiritual equality is closer to the core of things than all the inequalities.

factor in religious attitudes. Here the child is father to the adult perhaps more than in most other facets of personality. The religious biography of almost anyone would be likely to supply an example of the role of the social setting, and the thesis that the religious attitude is simply "a socially created design for living."

The role of individuality has also been found to be an important factor. A study of American college students showed that over half had shifted away from the belief system in which they had been raised.[4] Despite the importance of early training in the growth of the need of religion, a third of the students developed religious interest in the absence of such training. Attitudes are almost always to some degree unique. "The roots of religion are so numerous, the weight of their influence in individual lives so varied, and the forms of rational interpretation so endless, that uniformity . . . is impossible."[5]

A mentally mature person, a writer on personality suggests, should have a diversity of interests outside of the self. He also needs a unifying philosophy of life. The first of these goes with growth, the "expanding self"; the second means direction and coherence. A strong interest may give an order of priority for all other matters. It helps one to make decisions, gives zest to living and provides a refuge from small irritants and distresses. It raises self-esteem and enables one to establish his identity—to answer the question: Who am I?

A person "organized" in this way need not, of course, be religious. His dominating interest may be esthetic, scientific or altruistic. The religious personality, for Allport, is one in whom there is response to what is of *ultimate* meaning and value in the personal life. It must also be related to "what he regards as permanent or central in the nature of things."

Many personalities could provide examples for this statement, among them those eminent in various fields. A case often cited is that of Vincent van Gogh. Here the core motive was esthetic response to nature. The artist was highly sensitive to a variety of such subjects, which for him could be supremely beautiful. His life was strongly centered upon painting; all else, including food, rest and other basic needs, were always subordinate. Not only, however, was this interest central as an occupation; he regarded it as a greatly significant aspect of life itself. His response to nature was a form of worship; a conviction of the divinity of natural beauty was an integral part of his perception of it. It was a sacred thing, and his devotion was a dedication. Art and religion were here blended.[36]

Definitions of faith have ranged from the simple concept of belief not based upon proof to "believing what you know is not true," or "not *wanting* to know what is true (Nietzsche). Commitment may be greater than knowledge, and one may live actively by a decision resting on what seems "probable" rather than demonstrated. Many decisions require us to risk a degree of uncertainty.

Religious maturity, Allport suggests, may require that one build his life on a premise less than certain. Far more of our decisions than we realize rest on probability. "Some people . . . say they are unable to entertain religious propositions with less than full certainty, even though these same people commit themselves gladly to the probabilities of everyday life." [9] For those who must have a belief of some kind there is no other choice, where certainty is not possible, than to adopt a faith with incomplete supports. Here a logic somewhat like that of "Pascal's wager" may meet the need: if a belief in ultimate meaning helps heighten morale in daily living, one can only gain in holding it, for nothing is lost, here and now, if the belief is false.

In what is probably the best-known book on religion

by a psychologist, William James wrote that "the pivot around which the religious life . . . revolves, is the interest of the individual in his private personal destiny." [43] He emphasized, as does Allport, the variable meaning of religion for each person: for the "sick soul," deliverance; for the lonely, love and "home"; for the guilty, redemption. The most mature religious attitude is often a product of doubt and conflict.

James was unwilling to accept the view that the need of a belief in deity is a trait of the childhood of a society. In their weakness, fears and bereavements—so one theory proposed—people must have faith in a power to which they can turn with entreaty, for consolation, and, in desperation, even with demand. "To coerce the spiritual powers . . . to get them on our side, was, during enormous tracts of time, the one great object in our dealings with the natural world." [44] Religion in some cultures still contains some of this primitive kind of thinking.

The progress of science, this argument continues, has greatly changed man's status. In giving him not only an understanding of natural processes but in providing him with ways of controlling them it has brought him out of the role of helpless supplicant and given him the tools to survive on his own resources. Being so vastly more able to help himself than ever before, he now no longer needs to turn to religion as a dependent. For problems of every kind the technologies of science are available and this has altered man's morale and his image of himself. It has given him confidence in his abilities and in his initiative; he can face a future which is increasingly in his own hands. Eventually, in this view, religion will decline and vanish because the needs to which it ministered will be fulfilled without it. The childhood of the race will be ended. Mankind will have come of age.

James disagreed with this view of religion as no more than a "phase" through which a society must pass. He rejected it on grounds with which many students would agree today. Science, for all its achievements, represents but one interpretation of reality. Its concepts are basically abstractions from a much larger whole.* The larger whole includes, by far most importantly, individual experience in the sphere of religion. Such experience is in closer touch with the living core of reality, James believed, than the concepts and laws of science. In those laws "we deal only with the symbols of reality, but as soon as we deal with private and personal phenomena, we deal with reality in the completest sense of the term." [45] What we find in the "private and personal" sphere of religion is an *emotional* response that is more vital than anything science has to offer. The history of religion shows a great variety of interpretations but the feelings "are almost always the same—for Stoic, Christian, and Buddhist saints are practically indistinguishable in their lives." The feelings relate directly to conduct, and both are the truly essential elements in religion considered psychologically. The "faith-state" works; it has, and has always had, impressive power; it energizes; it "is a biological as well as a psychological condition."

Somewhere in my reading I once encountered a brief but memorable historical ancedote focused upon a Roman slave of the first century at the time when the great "good tidings" of Christianity were slowly beginning to spread. The slave, scarcely human in his vegetative existence as a

---

* In this brief survey a large place is given to James' study because the work of this great psychologist covers so many of the essentials of religious experience and dynamics. The writer agrees with another student in this area that "many leading personality scientists today have reached conclusions very similar to those reached by James nearly seventy years ago. . . . In some ways his insights are more relevant today than ever." [76]

laborer in the mines, was benumbed with toil, dumb with despair and misery. Then came the "gospel," which reached him as a proclamation of the worth and dignity of the individual, the hope of a great redemption, and the promise of a kingdom symbolized by the figure and the teachings of Christ. There followed an enormous lift in morale and stamina; a complete example of the doctrine that man can endure any *how* if he is given a *why*. James' stress on the "dynamogenic" value of religion could be justified by countless such examples, many of which he supplies himself.

What is it that sustains the faith-state; what is the evidence? Here again the subjective experience of the individual is crucial. The answer, for James, comes out of the great mass of documents on which his study is largely based. All of them show, he believes, that a person has become aware that his "ideal self" is part of a "*more* of the same quality, which is operative in the universe outside of him . . ." For some religions the "more" is, of course, deity itself, as a person. For others it may be simply an "ideal tendency embedded in the eternal structure of the world." [46]

Here psychology makes direct contact with religion by way of the *subconscious* sector of mental life. It is through this channel, deep within the larger self, that contact with the ideal force is made. "Whatever it may be on its farther side, the 'more' with which in religious experience we feel ourselves connected is on its hither side the subconscious continuation of our conscious life." [47]

Here James' treatment suggests a development which would link it closely with earlier discussion: that the "subconscious" represents, among other things, *the expression within individual experience* of the biological processes at the root of evolution. Man, and no other animal, is able to conceive of divinity and to feel that he makes contact with it. The biology of what has made him human must be the source of this vital element of his mental life. Only divinity, James might have said, could have bestowed upon man the gift of feeling its own presence.

The form of such "contact" experiences varies but tends to be esthetic. A fertile source of religious responses is the world of nature, not as the scientist perceives it but as the painter or the poet may sense it—the Van Goghs and the Wordsworths. From another and quite different region of experience an historian comes close to what James had in mind: "As we brood over the drama of history, we can hardly help feeling a depth of meaning beyond the reach of mere logic or science . . . and this fact of immediate experience always suggests the possibility that man is attuned to the Absolute, and in his history is fulfilling some superhuman purpose." [64]

Books on the psychology of religion commonly include discussion of the emotional factors in belief. Apart from the nature of evidence and the quality of reasoning, beliefs are influenced by needs, and it is agreed that in matters of religious belief the role of emotional need is unusually large. Several different kinds have been discussed by students of religious motivation. Belief in God may be seen as an expression of a "father complex," a dependent need persisting in the adult and rooted in the child's reliance on its male parent. "It is viewed as a form of nostalgia, a pathetic homesickness for the parental care of infancy." [52]

A person's frustrations and defeats may also incline him toward religion in search of grounds for a hope that his defeats will finally be redeemed, that there is a cosmic justice that will make restitution for what he has suffered. Religion may thus "dull the pain of a tragic existence."

Belief may be sustained in part by resentment, as in people with faith in the conviction that God will punish those who have wronged them (sometimes illustrated in the medieval fantasy that the blessed in heaven will be permitted to view and enjoy the tortures of the damned). It is obvious that these and similar emotional elements may be classed under the heading of wishful thinking, or needful believing.*

A number of writers on the psychology of religion have emphasized a central theme of this chapter: that *social* and religious motives are closely linked. A primary need of human life is a basic relationship with another person or persons. This need is also an essential of religious growth, religion itself being, in one view, "a search for meaningful relationships." A vital element in human behavior is *the need of a sustaining bond.* Everyone "hungers for relationships significant enough to invite his devotion and central enough to orient his striving. . . . To know a secure and satisfying relation with someone who loves is to have a basic pattern for religious experience of faith and love." [48] For religious growth the experience of a close social bond is the central basis of a religious attitude. Complete emotional security in such a bond is the matrix for a personal relationship with deity. This means that strong social bonds may in some measure satisfy the religious need it-

---

* Paul Johnson has pointed out, as have others, that atheism is often as much rooted in emotion as is theism. It is "by every test as much a belief as theism . . ." It may be seen as a revolt against authority and linked with Freudian theory; "if theism may be traced to the father complex, it is quite as logical to trace atheism to the Oedipus complex, a jealous desire to overthrow and supplant the father." [53] It may also be prompted in part by a self-assertive thrust of the ego, which gains elevation by scornful rejection of faiths as uncritically naive.

Another variety of atheism is seen in those who, driven into bitterness and indignation by the world's tragedies, are thereby emotionally reinforced in a judgment resting primarily on rational grounds.

self. The *emotional* factor in religious faith is essentially a social need.

In the large field of problems for which the services of a psychotherapist are commonly sought, the importance of the personal relationship with the therapist himself has steadily risen. Many professionals now regard it as of equal status with the techniques of treatment. Some have even concluded that most or all "mental" problems are themselves at core interpersonal in character. "In our time psychiatrists are increasingly viewing mental illness as disturbances of interpersonal relations, and particularly of communication." [49]

To perceive the therapist as not only knowledgeable but as an emotionally responsive human being may be of greater meaning to the patient than the technical tools of analysis and treatment. The quality of this personal relationship has come to be seen as primary rather than as incidental. The therapist who expresses esteem, warmth, concern and "fellow feeling" may be meeting the truly basic needs of his patient. The latter, in "his desperate feeling of estrangement . . . needs to be accepted by another person who is willing to enter into his suffering with him." [50] Carl Rogers writes: "There is . . . within the therapist, a profound experience of the underlying communality—should we say brotherhood—of man. As a result he feels toward the client a warm, positive, affectional reaction . . . the inevitable reaction on the part of the client is to relax, to let the warmth of liking by another person reduce the tension and fear involved in facing life." [74] Anton Boisen, long ago, suggested that the true root of mental illness was to be found in "the sense of isolation and estrangement" for which the treatment was "restoration to the fellowship of that *social* something which we call God." [13]

In his studies of emotional needs in human relationships

P. A. Sorokin has reviewed a number of areas of evidence demonstrating the "life-giving and life-sustaining" potency of these needs and of their fulfillment. The suicide rate, for example, rises and falls as emotional attachments diminish and increase in strength. "We know now that the main cause of suicide is psychosocial isolation of the individual, his state of being lonely in the human universe, not loving or caring for anybody and not being loved by anybody." [79] Regardless of uncertainty as to the best psychiatric method professionals agree, he observes, that the most important curative agent is the "empathy, sympathy, kindness and love established between the therapist and the patient."

The "transference" so basic to psychoanalytic treatment has been seen as essentially the formation of an emotional bond. "If the isolation . . . could be overcome, if contact and communication between the individual and at least one other person . . . could be established, the [patient] might be healed." [11] The relationship implied is at minimum one of acceptance, and may be increasingly positive in quality. "A patient in treatment . . . makes progress toward health in proportion . . . as he feels accepted and wanted by therapist, family and associates. Love received and love given comprise the best form of therapy." [51]

Many agree that the religious quest is an effort "to counteract isolation by relating oneself to a loving community. . . . *Religious seeking is a social experience* and its direction is outward bound to the ultimate relationship with God. . . . Religious faith is the deepening and enlarging of a trustworthy relationship between persons." [51] What might appear to be a blurring of the distinction between social and religious needs here is in fact an evidence of their close relationship.

At the emotional level they overlap and tend to merge.

There are many references of this kind in the literature of religious psychology. A student of the emotional experiences that occur in group therapy writes: "People are able to accept themselves and each other just as they are. Deep, genuine caring for others occurs, and people know what it means to love. Some of these experiences are so profound that they can be described as . . . religious." [80] Boisen, who knew at firsthand the estrangement of mental illness, has repeatedly stated that the essence of religious experience lies in the *social need which is met in the feeling of union with deity.* "Religious experience is rooted in the social nature of man. It is the sense of fellowship raised to the level of the abiding and universal. . . . It is the response to that in the universe upon which men feel dependent for love and for protection." * [14]

Foremost in definitions of human love is the urge to ensure the well-being of another person. There are many degrees of "caring," and "concern," all with the same mean-

---

* The experience of deity as a personal presence is evident in a statement by a member of one of the writer's therapy groups, a university student of twenty-two.

In one of his sermons our minister told us to think of God as "the friend at your side." This was the title of his sermon. It struck me because it summed up exactly what my own feelings had been for a long time. Whenever I thought of God I thought that *He* would be thinking of me at the same time because he would know that this was when I needed him. This was always a very great comfort to me. It meant that I would never be alone when I really needed someone, and that his "someone" was the Great Being Himself.

I've read somewhere that this kind of religious feeling is simply transferring to God the way you feel toward your father, but I'm certain there is more to it than this because I never felt this way about my father. I loved him, but he was away a great deal and I never felt the kind of closeness to him I feel about God. The strongest feeling I have about God is that *I'll never be really alone.*

"Religious man," observes an historian of religion (Mircea Eliade), "is never alone."

ing. After the life-preserving functions have been served, the strongest of needs is for love—so numberless students in the human sciences agree. If love is also the outstanding *emotional* attribute of deity, it is clear that the most effective "natural" means of meeting this need must lie in the corresponding human bond. "God is love," we are endlessly assured, and to love and *be loved* is the most summary statement of the basic human hunger. This is the essence of the relationship between the religious and the social need.*

Many have observed that a vital element in the emotional meaning of religious behavior is and has long been inherent in the *gathering together* of people in worship. The sense of community is sustaining in itself, quite apart from whatever comes from the relationship to deity. Much of the literature of religious psychology suggests that an intensified sense of community and of common purpose, whatever its source, may become strong enough to meet in large part the need that religion has traditionally fulfilled.

The view that religious and social needs are closely related is clear in some of the doctrines of the philosophy of *humanism*—to be later outlined—among them that "men who have believed in supernatural powers have not believed in them for their own sake, but for the human val-

---

* For those reliant on the God of tradition the idea that he may be partially replaceable by even the deepest and closest of human relationships will doubtless be dismissed at once as no solution to the problem of religious needs. For the image offered by the advocates of a limited deity this possibility may seem much less strained. A bond with a striving, purposeful but incomplete "fellow-sufferer" God is much closer, it would seem, to a human relationship which offers sympathetic support and a sense of united goal seeking. The common factors in the God of Whitehead, of James and Berdyaev make a concept far less godlike than that of the established Churches, but for that reason also much more nearly one whose emotional meaning may be approached in human closeness and collective strength.

ues of comfort, hope, and assurance that have been vividly associated with such belief." [20] The older faith is largely replaceable, in this philosophy, by "finding in the sense of . . . comradeship with one's fellows a more satisfying compensation for loss of the . . . illusory feeling that underneath are the everlasting arms of a divine protector." [19] A high degree of the *same kind* of emotional security that religion has provided may be found in interpersonal bonds.

At this point—in linkage with an earlier discussion—it may be seen that the view of the origins of behavior, including the most creative, as finally inherent in the root structures and processes of evolution and in the conditions of the individual life offers what may be the most basic of interpersonal bonds. That every person is a product of biological and social forces for which he is never more than a medium is the ultimate foundation of human *community*. The enormous gaps that separate the gifted from the ungifted, the fortunate from the unfortunate, "show only that some are the darlings and some the victims of 'circumstances beyond control.' " The vast differences in the quality of individual lives is no more basic a reality than that we are all in large part outcomes of unknown sources.

It is on this ground that one could say to a "superior": You have been more favored, yet we are alike in that neither of us, if total analysis could be made, had a choice in what we are, and that it is beyond any issue of merit that life's bonuses come to some far more than to others. What we have in common is more fundamental than our differences, and on this deepest ground the great ones of the world are brothers of the most wretched. Here may be the one salvageable meaning of the otherwise blatant untruth that all are created equal.

The sense of community has itself played a vital role in

religion from the beginning, shown in the early Judeo-Christian Church. "So great was the sense of mutual participation and the dependence of each person on the life of the whole, that St. Paul could compare the church to a single organism." [12] The vital role of the fellowship bond in religious gatherings and practices has often been stressed in the literature of religious psychology. It is suggested that much of the strength that religion brings into life comes out of the shared experiences of religious communion and the kinship feelings rooted in common beliefs.* We conclude that for many the chief emotional support in religious participation may be social rather than doctrinal, or that while the framework may be doctrinal the essential support is social and emotional. This is only to propose that a large part of the security and the lift in morale that religion has supplied may finally be replaced by the basic fellowship sentiment combined with confidence that man's capacity to master his problems and to use that mastery to aid his fellows will give him much of what religion has hitherto provided.

A psychologist who believes that "we have lost the strong sense of community and commitment which characterized early Christianity and have become disastrously individualistic, independent, and isolated," notes that contemporary communism is effectively employing the methods of the early Christian church.[62] "In both instances there is a marked sense of 'community' and tremendous camaraderie." Another notes that the spiritual and social

---

* "All religion is rooted in social feelings; it is something *shared* with others, and involves *community* of ideals and cooperative activities. Man is a social being, and religion is an expression of his social nature. In its great vision of the Brotherhood of Man, it is the highest expression of man's capacity for extending his social ties . . . the widest of all the appeals that religion makes is to man's craving for companionship. . . . The sense of fellowship . . . permeates the religious life." [73]

unity achieved by religion during the Middle Ages was shattered by the growth of Protestantism, scientific technology and industrialization. The cost of these advances was the sacrifice of community. "A terrible loneliness and a sense of isolation" are among the consequences. "In our present culture, many of the human bonds of community, bonds seen so necessary to the spirit as to be constitutive of all that is humanly natural, have come apart." [90]

A study of the sources of the contemporary "student revolution" or counterculture resulted in a list of different aims of the trend, among which were: cooperation rather than competition; community rather than individualism; encouragement of natural expression and rejection of artifice; the discovery of one's individuality; and the attempt to live, so far as possible, in groups based on congeniality.[91]

In humanistic writings the distinction between religious and nonreligious motivation loses much of its sharpness. So far as any major interest is felt as deeply and personally meaningful it may be the basis of an *emotionally* "religious" life, regardless of the presence or absence of faith in the orthodox sense. A close friendship, if it raises morale and evokes feelings of acceptance, confidence and security, may help toward the kind of need to which religion proper has always sought to minister. The values of a religious life may coincide with those of other modes of living in terms of depth of interest and dedication, and this may be true independently of doctrinal concerns.

In a book on help for emotional problems through the interaction of people in groups (group therapy), Prof. O. H. Mowrer writes: "Anyone goes mad who goes too far alone." Many psychologists, including the writer, believe that the most important discovery of this century in the treatment of emotional problems is that great benefits in insight and morale are possible when small groups meet to pool their resources on problems of anxiety, depression, loneliness and guilt. What *kind* of social experience this means is the theme of this section and one of the major themes of this chapter. Mowrer's statement that "we cannot find salvation *alone*," that it must be sought in certain relationships with others, may sound trite as it stands. It can have value only when given a new meaning.

Much of group therapy is geared to the relief of feelings of guilt and isolation. Man is "preeminently a social creature whose greatest and most devastating anguish is experienced, not in physical pain or biological deprivation, but when he feels alienated . . ." When a person can acknowledge guilt in a group setting, marked emotional benefit may follow. Willingness to reveal oneself is necessary. Complete honesty in this sense is an essential of emotional health.

Far more, however, may follow upon such self-revelation. It may be a means to "salvation" of a much larger and deeper kind. Confession may at outset mark the removal of all defensive masking, or shielding. It has a vitally important social meaning, namely: "I am willing to let you know me as I truly am; to set aside the barriers of pretense, of ego protection. I am willing to open my self to you so that we may become closer to each other." The origin of the open hand in greeting, it is said, was to testify that it held no weapon. Confession may be seen as a similar gesture, to signal that there is to be no contest of egos, no maneuvering for power or status. It can be a symbol which acknowledges a fundamental fellowship.

Confession may relieve guilt, but its positive side may be of far greater import in opening the way to a kind of communication which can bring with it a strength related to some of the issues introduced at the beginning of this book. Preliminary to it, however, is a uniquely fruitful kind of attitude and insight. The attitude is a generalized mental set toward all other persons. The insight is a realization of certain *basic identities* with others. Both are illustrated in a case study which is unusual only in its clarity and coherence of statement.

The subject is a man of fifty-one, a successful journalist who lives alone, being childless and having lost his wife a year before the account that follows, and concerns his recovery from severe depression.

The loss of my wife was by far the greatest emotional shock of my life. My emotional dependence on my wife had been great. We were very close and compatible; we had been married 22 years.

The bond was so close that we had little need of others. We had little social life and no really close friendships. I had no one to turn to who might have helped ease the shock. I felt abandoned and quite lost. For weeks I was unable to work; I had some suicidal thoughts. I knew that I should make some moves, that I should get "back in circulation" or travel, but was too paralyzed with depression and grief to make a beginning. Apart from moving from our home into an apartment I was able to do little or nothing.

I saw a psychiatrist, not for the usual treatment but to get a prescription for an antidepressant. He recommended group therapy. His argument was that I had settled all my need of human relationships on one person and so had nothing in reserve. He said that such a close marriage could be very satisfying but that there was always a danger of severe stress if it should be threatened in any way, and most of all by loss through death. My mistake had been to let my marriage become too "exclusive"; my social life was too narrow. I had become a "social isolate."

I began group therapy and it led to what I can say was one of the most important experiences of my life. It was slow in coming and more than once I was on the brink of dropping out, but I think this was mainly because of my depression. I was simply too low to respond.

The group had been meeting for several months before I started. I was greatly impressed from the beginning by something I had never seen before. I had never seen people reveal themselves with such honesty. They took things in stride I would have thought would be an ordeal to talk about. There was much discussion of insecurity. These people admitted being confused, afraid and frustrated with frankness I would never have thought possible.

This was all new to me. It was as if they were saying: this is how I really am. It was a kind of honesty that was almost like nakedness. It showed that they expected to be accepted as they were, that they trusted each other. They knew that no one would take advantage. They were getting into closer contact. I remember having the thought—how wonderful it would be if everybody could be this way all the time. It would be like living in a different world. As if we all belonged to an enormous yet closely knit family.

The most important experience I had is hard to explain. It involved my wife in relation to other people. She was a very fine person, the finest I have ever known; kind and loving, honest and loyal, and many other things. I had tremendous sympathy with her. I really thought of her as unique, not only that no one could take her place but that no one could possibly deserve my love as much as she did.

It was through the group that I began to see that this was not true. My wife was of course not unique. I think the essence of my "insight" was that it dawned on me that the traits I valued and loved in her were present in many others *to some degree*. That there were others as worthy of being loved as she was if I knew them as I knew her, or at least knew them well. My experience of loving and of emotional response to others had been too narrow. I had been blind to the inner selves of others. I didn't realize that there were many, men as well as women, who could mean to some degree what my wife meant. Sex, by the way, has nothing to do with it. It is simply the need for closeness with another human being. It is simply responding to them and feeling they are responding to us. If the feeling is strong enough I suppose it could be called love, but I think that fellow-feeling is better, or friendship-love.

I have wondered whether differences between people are really so important. I'm sure they mean something, but what is more important is finding someone we can relate to enough to be able to care about them. This counts for more than what they look like, or education, or talents, and so on. Finally, I guess, to know that we are acceptable and maybe even lovable to a few people, or even to one person—this is the whole of it.

I feel certain now, looking back on it, that the loss of my wife would have been much less a shock if I had had either a firm religion or a few strong bonds with others.

When I left the group I was ready, as I never had been before, to open up to people. I was far more outgoing and socially minded than I had ever been before.

Early during his depression this man turned to religion for the first time in his life. "It was desperation. It was grasping at straws. All I really wanted was something that would give me hope that I would see my wife again. It helped a little, but it was unstable and did not last. Just words I had heard before. I needed something more solid. I envied people who had faith. I wanted to believe but I just couldn't manage it."

In the group he found, first of all, a mood in harmony with his own—others like himself unhappy in some way and seeking supports. The therapist emphasized that they were there for a joint venture in understanding themselves and others; a sense of "common cause" was encouraged. It was also stressed that while there were many thousands in groups of this kind, these were but a fraction of the people who needed and would benefit from group membership, but who because of resistance, or circumstances or lack of awareness of their needs had failed to seek this kind of help.

The turning point in this instance was the subject's insight that his feelings for his wife were potentially *transferable*, to some degree, to others. On one occasion he expressed this clearly within the group. "Sometimes, when I'd hear of a misfortune to somebody, it would register very little. It would not really touch me. Then I would imagine the same thing happening to my wife and I'd know how I'd feel, that it would be anguish. Then I would have the thought that the person it happened to could be just as fine and worthy as my wife. Someone who loved that person would be suffering just as I would suffer. Then I would know that deep down we are all alike, that we can all feel for each other in the same way." *

The result was an expansion of feeling, or of the capacity for emotional participation in the lives of others; essentially the discovery that "they are also *me's.*" "Insight" here included recognition that impressions of uniqueness in a personal attachment are often illusory. Individuality may be irreplaceable, but participation is possible in a wide range of individualities so far as there is awareness of basic identities. †

---

* Allport has described similar insights regarding the sense of personal worth. One asks himself: "If I am acutely self-conscious and disposed to brook no lese majesty against my person, are not others . . . equally attached to their egos? And thus . . . I gradually come to value whatever makes for the conservation of personal integrity anywhere. . . . *Where once only my personal life was the supreme value, I now acknowledge the worth of any person.*" [6]

† Santayana once wrote: "Love is . . . much less exacting than it thinks itself. Nine-tenths of its causes are in the lover, for one-tenth that may be in the object. Were the latter not accidentally at hand, an almost identical passion would probably have been felt for someone else . . ." [77] This statement, applied (as it originally was) to the "romantic" type of attraction may be doubted, but for love in its far different and broader nonsexual connotation it may approach an essential truth.

It is the main thesis of this section that certain kinds of social-emotional states are importantly related to the problems which may follow upon the loss or weakening of religious faith. The emotional linkage between religious and social behavior has been long established. Experiences which may be vitally helpful in a social context are clearly evident in what is now familiarly known as group therapy.

During recent decades a new form of therapy group has developed. Earlier work of this kind was focused upon emotional problems ranging from mild neuroses to psychotic states. For the "new group therapy," whose growth has been extraordinarily rapid, the emphasis is not upon the treatment of "mental ills" but upon personal development; enrichment of the personality rather than repair of defects; on the improvement of social skills; and above all upon the emotional value of closer relationships. Many who attend the new groups feel the need of ability to more fully *open* themselves socially and to enter into the emotional lives of others with greater freedom and to greater depth.*

There are strong barriers to release of this kind, and here such terms as "facade building," "ego armour," "masking" and "shielding" are much in use. We live in a society in which self-editing for the maintenance of "front" is habitual in nearly everyone. "The highly competitive American

---

* Carl Rogers has characterized the group movement, under its various names, as "the most rapidly spreading *social* invention of the century, and probably the most potent." He emphasizes that it has been a spontaneous expression of the *needs of people*, rather than of any established institution or profession. The range of individuals involved is from corporation presidents, college faculties and students, industrial managers, school administrators and teachers, to dropouts, drug addicts, alcoholics, delinquents and imprisoned criminals. Geographically the movement has spread from Maine to California, and through several European countries, Australia and Japan. (Rogers, C. *Carl Rogers on Encounter Groups.* New York: Harper and Row, Publishers, Incorporated (Harrow Books), 1973, pp. 1–2.)

culture . . . encourages facade-building. The successful man . . . too often strives to protect his public image at all cost. If he has doubts about his adequacy, he swallows them and maintains constant vigilance lest any personal uncertainty or discomfort slip through." [88]

In the new groups, most commonly known as "T-groups" (T for training, as in "human-relations training groups"), also as "encounter," human-relations or "awareness" groups, effort is made to abandon all the devices which stand in the way of honest human communication.

All accoutrements which in the outside world symbolize success and normality are deposited at the door of the T-group. Individuals are no longer rewarded for their material success, for their hierarchical position, for their unruffled aplomb, for their efficiency, or for their expertise in their area of specialization; instead they are exposed to the totally different values of the T-group, in which they are rewarded for interpersonal honesty and for the disclosure of self-doubts and perceived weaknesses. Gradually they discover that . . . the facade is not only unnecessary but an encumbrance.* [89]

In the T-group the members learn that certain assumptions on which they have lived all their lives are false; for

---

* In one statement the T-group is defined as having as its goal an experience in which what is learned is continuously created by the group activity itself.[16] It comes through the interaction of the members themselves rather than from a teacher or leader. All the factors that normally tend toward the mental separation of individuals: defensiveness, withdrawal, fear and distrust are reduced. Gradually the members discover that openness in sharing feelings and willingness to give and receive entail little or no risk. Instead, they lead to easier communication and gains in self-discovery.

The focus tends to be on here-and-now interests, and events within the group itself. Problems of socializing and loneliness, the ability to express and receive affection and love, the search for identity, may be discussed.

example, that giving up defenses and lowering the facade must mean humiliation, rejection or loss of status. Instead, they find themselves fully accepted on the basis of their authentic selves. As compensations, the feeling of isolation is diminished and a lift in self-esteem comes with the discovery of the near universality of personal insecurities.*

Much of traditional group therapy centered upon the problems of the neurotic. The more recent movement was and is designed for the alienated, the socially inept, the inhibited, the holdback, the person chronically unable to release whatever socially oriented impulses he possesses. It is in part also a reaction to the impersonality of our society and to the weakening of the institutions and patterns which have in the past met the need for emotional closeness.

A recent sociological writer has vividly described the effect of increasing mobility on the character of contacts between people.[83] They become shallow, transient and *fractional* in the sense that too often only a small part of

---

* The "Consciousness III" mentality described by Charles Reich (*The Greening of America*) coincides well with some of the major objectives of the encounter group movement, the aim being to remove the barriers imposed by the awareness of *status* in human relationships. It does not judge the individual but accepts him in his uniqueness. It "postulates the absolute worth of every human being—every self." Relationships based solely on role and function are rejected, and there is no virtue in obligations discharged "when the feeling is gone." People of Consciousness III "are in no hurry to find out another person's background, schools, achievements, as a means of knowing him . . ." All are in central essence brothers, "all belong to the same family, whether they have met each other or not." More vital than status, roles, competitive advantage, is "the warmth of the 'circle of affection' in which men join hands."

Such an ideal, in the deepest sense democratic and Christian, is directly opposed to the present mental structure of much of our society, in which, as some have suggested, the "psychopathic strain" in its egoistic, predatory and aggressive aspects has become the preferred model.

the total person is known. It is the part involved in some specialized function or service. Combined with loss or weakening of religious faith, this kind of impersonality may account for much of the profound feelings of aloneness and "anomie" so widely prevalent.*

In much of the literature of the new therapy the emphasis falls on contact with the *essential* person. This is the "self" that makes the core of emotional needs and major values, apart from all marginal and conventional facets of personality. It is through recognition and sharing of these core elements that vital identifications are made. Without them there can be no access of strength in awareness of common selfhood. There will be no lift in spirit through felt unity.

So far as our society can be described as facade building, vigilant against self-revelation and tending to sacrifice spontaneity for the unruffled front, it has been contrasted with an aspect of Russian culture. A close observer notes in these people "a fundamental loyalty to one's own feelings"; the Russian "delights in people who are both . . . sensitive in appreciating other people's moods and situations and . . . full of sympathetic response." The pretences

---

* What Dostoevsky wrote over a century ago of pre-revolutionary Russian society might apply well to contemporary America:

All mankind in our age have split up into units, they all keep apart, each in his own groove; each one holds aloof, hides himself and hides what he has from the rest, and he ends by being repelled by others and repelling them. . . . [Each] is accustomed to rely upon himself alone and to cut himself off from the whole; he has trained himself not to believe in the help of others . . . and only trembles for fear he should lose his money and the privileges that he has won for himself. Everywhere in these days men have . . . ceased to undrstand that the true security is to be found in social solidarity rather than in isolated individual effort. But this terrible individualism must inevitably have an end, and all will suddenly understand how unnaturally they are separated from one another. . . . [Then] people will marvel that they have sat so long in darkness without seeing the light.[24]

so common to our social intercourse are absent; there is "respect for an expression of genuine personal feeling." Freedom from self-importance is stressed; the Russian has a sense of dignity but does not "stand on it." Self-confidence is rooted in security of acceptance. There is a strong sense of belonging to the national family, a "largely unconscious sense of community"; no English word, we are told, describes "the fundamental Russian quality of behaving according to one's feelings." [59]

A religious attitude has been suggested as having a large role in this community-mindedness. Being gathered together is "an essential condition of blessedness. . . . To experience profoundly this feeling of fellowship with even the dirtiest and most lowly one must attend one of the Easter Eve services. . . . All quarrels are to be forgiven, all men truly made brethren at this great ceremony. . . . Today, when few Russians attend church regularly, enormous numbers still join in the Easter service." [59] In the context of nonreligious modes of "salvation" it has often been suggested that socialist and communist movements in their more democratic and humanitarian aspects may help greatly to meet the social-emotional needs which traditional religion has sought to fulfill. "Such secularized quasi-religious movements offer a kind of belongingness; they satisfy to some degree the quest for community." To those who feel uprooted or alienated they may "bring the community and sense of worth and meaning formerly associated with religious movements." [72]

An important meaning of the new group movement is that it provides contacts for persons whose need, mood and mental set are frankly and often intensely concerned with basic problems of living, with the development of a personal philosophy and with issues of "ultimate concern." Apart from the collective search for a rationale for confronting and coping with individual problems such group efforts help to meet the *emotional* needs of people who have failed to find support in religion or satisfaction in the values of our society. They have often failed, too, to find understanding in friends and relatives less affected by similar doubts and malaise of spirit.

Among them are some who consciously hope for a new approach to living, a different attitude, an "enlightenment" of some kind. It is often clear, however, that others come for a different reason. It is not for communication but for "communion." They share the discussion, but for them the individual is more important than the topic. Interest tends to shift away from the content of dialogue toward the person-to-person contact. The difference is sometimes apparent in the tone of voice and in the expression of the eyes. In those in search of insights the gaze tends to be abstracted or unfocused, while the ones primarily seeking a personal relationship are more active in conveying extroverted interest and warmth of feeling.

Some group members are clearly in quest of friendships or a love relationship, or both. Their responses are discriminating and tend to be directed toward particular persons. In others, more concerned with the group as a whole, much of the expression of emotional needs tends to fall largely within the three general headings of sharing, acceptance and direct help of some kind. Illustrative "testimonials" of each of these types follow:

I'm not sure I can explain the effect of sharing in the problems of the group except that it definitely reduced my feeling of being unfortunate. By that I mean looking at others or hearing about them and thinking they are better off, that they don't have the frustrations and disappointments I've had; that they are more successful. Thoughts like these made me bitter and depressed.

It was a revelation when the therapist said there were many hundreds of groups like ours all over the country. An enormous number of people had problems of the kind we talked about, like being afraid and not having confidence and wondering what life is all about. Often the thought came to me, that *there are a lot of us.* There must be thousands too who needed this kind of experience and did not know about groups like this. The group meant that *we are finding each other.* Knowing we are all going through it and that we can do it together is what counted.

* * *

From the beginning I felt accepted by the group, but my idea of what it meant changed. At first I thought it was just part of the therapy, that it was understood as the way everybody should act regardless of how they felt. Later I decided it was just an impression I was giving them, and that if they really knew me they would think differently about me and probably treat me differently. This, by the way, is an example of my habit of thinking about myself.

Finally it dawned on me that I really was accepted by the group and that it would mean that I was actually an acceptable person. I began to feel likeable and as if I had something to give, something that interested people. This helped me more than anything else that happened. I felt I had rejoined the human race. I knew what belonging meant for the first time.

* * *

After about six months of meetings I began to notice that I would think of the group as where I might get help apart from therapy. I don't mean anything direct or material. Once when I had to go to the hospital for some minor surgery I panicked a little and a girl in the group went with me. Later I did some baby-sitting for her. I began to feel that if I had a problem that any other person could possibly help me with, that the group would at least try, or that somebody in the group would try. During one meeting somebody made a joke about our being a "mutual aid society," but I think there was some truth in it. I'm sure that one of the things the group meant to me was that it was *someone to turn to* even if it meant only someone concerned enough to listen and perhaps come up with an idea. It was all really about the same thing as knowing people will help each other as they do in giving to charity or giving blood and doing volunteer work, only this was a more personal and intimate feeling.

Another illustrative case may be included to show the effect of group experience on the philosophy of values; in this instance a change from competition for excellence to a deep sense of fellowship with others.

I was an outstanding student in elementary school and did very well in high school. I felt I was headed for a high place in the world. In college it was very different. It seemed as if there were hundreds as smart as I was, or smarter. It dawned on me that I was really just another student and mediocre by college standards. I lost all my feeling of being somebody special. I became very depressed and at one time almost suicidal. The college counselor recommended that I join a therapy group.

What helped most in the group was that I saw that my problem was largely a matter of values. It had meant so much to feel I was superior. In the group I realized there were other ways of looking at things. Feeling fully accepted as part of something bigger can mean a great deal too. Feeling you're great may not be always the best thing there is. It is still pretty painful at times to know I'm really just run of the mill, but then I keep telling myself that having close friendships on a basis of equality can make up for what I missed. Perhaps in the long run being close to people and having good companionship is as good as being superior.

A final example may be offered to show that the gains from supportive social experiences in the group setting may be almost entirely emotional and free of events classed as "insight." It also illustrates, as do many comparable documents, the finding that the loss of a marital partner "is almost universally regarded as the single most impactful change that can befall a person in the normal course of his life." [84]

The subject is a nonneurotic male of fifty-two, a careerist in the insurance field, who has lived for over a year in a residential hotel since becoming a widower.

After my wife died I went through what I expect is a common experience; I didn't realize how much she had meant to me until after she was gone. I had taken married life pretty much for granted. After a few months I began to feel less depressed but there was an emptiness that continued. It was in the evenings I felt it most. At work I managed pretty well.

Some visits with my married daughters helped and I once thought of moving to the town where one of them lived, but decided against it when I realized that her life was well filled with her own family and friends. I could see that after a while there would be no real place for me.

I was drifting along in a rather aimless way, still depressed and at times feeling like a "zombie"—just going through the motions of living without any zest in anything. All my feelings were shallow. The turning point came when I heard of a minister of a Universalist church who had meetings that had something to do with emotional problems. The meetings themselves were not religious, so I was told, and that is when I got curious.

There were about a dozen people in the group, mostly middle-aged. They would probably be called middle class, or a bit better, and probably above the average in intelligence, judging from the way they talked.

At first I was disappointed in what seemed to be the aimlessness of the discussion. I couldn't see that they were headed anywhere in particular. The minister was usually there but he offered little in the way of guidance, mostly letting the talk drift. There was a lot of small talk, although it usually had something to do with personal problems or experiences. Nobody there seemed to be in a really bad way. Nobody in serious trouble, or if there was it didn't show. I felt accepted from the beginning. Nobody asked why I had come.

I remember having the thought several times that these people don't come here just for this kind of talk. They must have some other reason for coming and they must be getting something else out of this. For a while I could not say what it was.

There seemed to be two levels of what was going on. One was on the surface and the other was deeper, and I got the feeling that this was the real one, that brought them there. Something was going on that nobody was talking about, yet this was why these people were coming week after week.

We sometimes went to a coffee shop after the meetings and one night I had a few minutes alone with the minister. I asked him, "What is this all about, really?" He said the discussion itself was not often very important. He said "You'll find there is a certain strength that comes out of it, nevertheless." He said it's something you sense, that people simply need the presence of others at times, or a deeper level, that there is a fellowship between *real selves*. He said that when you get down to basics there is a feeling of kinship, and that this is where the strength comes from.

I got acquainted with a woman in the group whose husband was in a mental hospital with some kind of incurable brain disease. She seemed to have the same kind of feeling about the group. I think the "kinship" feeling was strong between us. I began to see her outside the meetings. There was also a man in the group about my age that I began to spend time with. We had some reading interests in common. I began to feel close to him too. I think I felt the same way about both these people. At times I would embrace Elsie and kiss her but there was no sex involved in it. I could embrace her only because she was a woman, but I felt the same way about the man. It was really part of the same feeling I had for the group itself, only more concentrated.

The group and these two friendships made me feel that I had some bonds. Somewhere in my reading I remember a saying that everyone needs a "somewhere" to go. Perhaps this really meant a "someone" to go to. I suppose most people know this, or take it for granted, but for me it was really a kind of discovery. These relationships could not mean as much to me as my marriage, but they were the closest thing to it. They seemed to satisfy the same kind of need.

It is obvious that in the experience thus described much more than "social presence" was active. There is such presence in many other social situations which are devoid of therapeutic value. What is essential here is that there is a level of communication which corresponds to the social aspect of the religious need. Such encounter groups—and those related to them, by whatever name—are the only human gatherings in which these needs provide the primary motive and structure.

The minister's reference to a "communion" is not uncommon in meetings of this kind. It is as if to say: We are met to seek to find in each other, or collectively, a more meaningful way of living, or at least of confronting life. Morale is elevated in finding oneself needed and in being able to meet the needs of others. The "kinship" experience, while not the same in quality in everyone, is at core a sensing of basic identity with others; thus, this person is at times, like myself, lost and afraid, and in this we are truly brothers, victims of the same mystery and confronted with the same questions.

A selective factor operates here to some extent, as everywhere else. For all that we grant our common humanity and willingness to accept others on this basis, this awareness will vary markedly between persons. Interests in common, emotional expression, intellectual level, physical traits, are doubtless among the grounds of selection. One cannot be drawn in this way to everyone, any more than one can like everyone or be liked by all.

The use of illustrative material from group therapy means only that the *kind* of social experience which meets a vital part of the religious need is most clearly evident here. It need hardly be said that it is not limited to such meetings. It may be active in almost any social context. The seeking which motivates the new group movement is often active, though not always consciously, in gatherings in which the formal purposes are quite different. The "social-emotional" need, commonly incidental in other settings, may yet be primary. The "T" or encounter groups are unique among all human associations in that nowhere else are such needs acknowledged and made explicit. Nowhere else can an individual be brought to the point of stating, without fear of uncomfortable consequences: I am here because I am in a special sense lonely for a certain kind of support, because there are barriers between myself and others which I must breach if I am to overcome my depression, anxiety, emptiness or isolation.

Two widely different attitudes may be taken toward another person, or two ways of regarding him. I may see him as an *object*, a tool to be used, a means to an end, a mere source of pleasure. My attitude toward him may in this respect differ little from that toward an animal; the person is only more complex and must be differently dealt with.

He may also be perceived, or *realized*, as in essentials an "approximation" of myself. My thoughts of him might then be expressed thus: Since this person and I are both human, there must be fundamental likenesses, even identities, between us, and these are more important than the differences. Our thoughts, talent and abilities may differ, but his *feelings* about himself, his anxieties, frustrations and distresses, may be much like my own. He may experience his needs as I do mine, and they may be as important to him as mine are to me. I may gain something from him, but must never forget that he has rights which I must respect. There must be mutuality in my dealings with him. To merely use him would be a violation and a disloyalty.*

Gordon Allport has applied the term "decentering" to the process whereby a child becomes able to comprehend that children of other countries, for example, may think of their homelands as he does his own. He is finally able to sense this across domestic lines and to regard himself as a member of a larger social unit. To feel "at one," or *as* one, with another or others, when it means grasping the mutuality of an experience, may also be seen as a form of decentering. It is to create, however briefly, an alter ego, or participating self. The need for such sharing, when it becomes deeply habitual, is well expressed in the often-quoted line: "Beauty viewed without the beloved is like a sword through the heart."

The widely current "I-Thou" concept of Martin Buber offers a helpful symbol here. His "I-*It*" relationship involves another only as an object; it is emotionally detached and manipulative. The I-*Thou* relationship, far different in quality, includes a *concerned* interest in another, and tends

* Writing of "The World of Things and the World of Persons," Paul Tournier has expressed a similar theme, with illustrations from the relationship between physician and patient.[86] This, to be most fruitful, must be one of "partners in a dialogue." "I allow my person to be discovered and known, and at the same time discover and know the person of my patient." In this mutual revelation of the self there is a basic person-to-person contact which makes the participants *equals* at the human level, whatever may be the differences in status otherwise.

to center on the experience of identity. The command-ment to "love thy neighbor as thyself" here means essen-tially to value one's neighbor as *a* self. So far as we relate to him in this way we feel *responsibility* toward him. His needs are as important as our own because his being is in the deepest sense one with our own.[17, 18]

The distinction between the other person as object and as self is broad in scope. For the predatory animal the vic-tim is an object; this is also largely true of the human pre-dator and helps to explain his callousness, especially when the victim is of a different race or culture. Some of the brutalities of conquest become more understandable if we assume a basic difference between perception of members of one's own group and those of other groups. This is often reported by students of primitives: the social virtues are practices limited to the same tribe but are suspended in re-lation to others. The insider is a self; the outsider an ob-ject.

The history of slavery is rich in examples. In Flaubert's *Salammbô* Hamilcar Barca is startled at an expression of grief on the part of one of his slaves, who has been in-formed that he must sacrifice his child. Hamilcar was ap-parently unaware that a slave might have even so elemental an emotion as parental love. The attitude of Europeans—and Americans—toward the trade in African slaves would provide more modern cases; likewise that of the criminal and the psychopath toward their prey.

Tolstoy, in *Anna Karenina*, makes this kind of percep-tion clear, likewise the way it may affect its "victim." With reference to the character Vronsky he writes:

He looked at people as if they were things. A nervous young man . . . sitting opposite, began to detest him for that look. The young man asked him for a light, addressed a few remarks to him, and even pushed against him to make him feel that he was not a thing but a man, but Vronsky continued to look at him as if he were a lamppost, and the young man kept pulling faces, feeling that he was losing self-control under the strain of this refusal to regard him as a human being.[85]

When one of the writer's counselees stated, "I believe in God and my husband, and there is no great difference in the feelings," she was not seeking to exalt her mate's character. She meant only that her faith in both was unqualified and that her feelings of dependency were similar. The subject of one of our case studies expressed a comparable sentiment in his recognition that the loss of his wife would have been less traumatic had he had the support of *either* religion *or* strong bonds with others. A wealth of clinical evidence confirms the view that the emotional response to a personal deity may be close to that basic to interpersonal relationships *when these contain to a high degree the quality of emotional identification.*

All such reports serve further as testimonials to Buber's statement that God for him means not a "principle" or an "idea" but "Him who—whatever else he may be—enters into a direct relation with us men . . . and thus makes it possible for us to enter into a direct relation with him." [17] While the concept of God as a personal being falls far short of defining him completely, "it is both permitted and necessary to say that God is *also* a Person." *

The emphasis in this section on the potentials of the kind of interpersonal bonds illustrated is based on the conviction, growing out of over twenty years of clinical work

---

* The social element in religious assembly itself is often illustrated. Thus: "In church I am making contact with God, but there is a good feeling too in meeting my neighbors and knowing we have all got our minds on the fundamentals of what life is about and what we are here for. Like the minister said, if we are children of God we are all related to each other and that means we should have a feeling of belonging with each other."

as well as copious testimony in the related psychological literature, that these, as no other, provide the most essential of all morale-building factors for those in need of such support. They are in this respect far more effective than those based on shared interests, on exchange of services or on amorous attraction and attachment. It is our thesis that they come closer than any other source to providing the kind of emotional fulfillment associated with religion. They offer the best "earthly substitute" for traditional faiths.

* * * * * *

The term "religious" is often loosely used for interests and activities that have deep meaning and inspire dedication As an adjective it may denote, as John Dewey has pointed out, attitudes "that may be taken toward any object and every proposed end or ideal." In this sense there is "religious" devotion to art, or to science or to a "cause." It may be a quality of almost any kind of experience.

Dewey tells of a writer who states:

I broke down from overwork and soon came to the verge of nervous prostration. One morning after a long and sleepless night . . . I resolved to stop drawing upon myself . . . and begin drawing upon God. I determined to set apart a quiet time every day in which I could relate my life to its ultimate source, regain the consciousness that in God I live, move and have my being. That was thirty years ago. Since then I have had . . . not one hour of darkness or despair.[21]

There are also, Dewey believes, *non*religious experiences which may be closely similar in effect in that they organize and strengthen a person's attitude toward the stresses of life. One may discover what is for him the highest value in a career or in certain human relationships. He may find a philosophy of some kind for meeting misfortunes. Whatever the character of the event or peak experience (Maslow), stresses are thereafter met, and decisions made with greater poise and security. The insight or adjustment leads to a new and more courageous approach to problems and challenges.

The meaning of a religious experience, it is suggested, "is not inherent in the experience itself. It is derived from the culture with which a particular person has been imbued." In the example given, this meaning was traditional. "For having been brought up in the Christian religion, its subject interprets it in the terms of the personal God characteristic of that religion." [22] For Dewey the "religious" quality of the experience lies in its emotional effects rather than in the "manner and causes of its production." The effect may come about in a variety of ways in different persons. "It is sometimes brought about by devotion to a cause; sometimes by a passage of poetry that opens a new perspective; sometimes . . . through philosophical reflection." An artist may feel that his subjects are symbols of the divine as well as patterns of form and color. It does not matter that the symbols are no more than projections of the artist's own beliefs or longings. The meanings and feelings are "religious" in this usage if they are vital enough to give zest to daily activities and if the artist feels himself fulfilled. They may also provide a buffer against shocks and distresses.*

* Referring to changes in personal orientation which so steady a person emotionally as to enable him to "endure unperturbed through the buffetings of fortune," Dewey writes: "It is the claim of religions that they effect this . . . change in attitude. I should like to turn the statement around and say that whenever this change takes place there is a definitely religious attitude." [23]

Many would not accept such an experience as religious even though they might concede that for some its effects could be comparable to those of traditional faiths. It must be recognized, nonetheless, that nonreligious motivations may bring zest, purpose and stamina enough to make the effects comparable to those of religion.

Strong interests, when they express central life values, may function as sources of "religious" motivation, in Dewey's sense. They may be vocational or avocational, marital, or social. Examples were often encountered by the writer in the course of counseling experiences with university students.

A couple of weeks after I was notified that a short story I wrote had been accepted for publication I learned that I had been turned down for membership in a fraternity. Ordinarily that would have really crushed me, yet I took the jolt in stride. It hurt, but I recovered so quickly that it surprised me.

I know that it was the story acceptance that made the difference. It enthused me and raised my confidence so much that hardly anything could have shaken it. Making a beginning in literature meant so much to me and gave me such a lift that it was like wearing armour. I felt strong enough to take almost anything.

* * * *

When I learned I was a diabetic and would have to go on a diet and take medication all the time I felt at first like it was the end of the world, that I was a seriously handicapped person and almost an invalid. I became very depressed. What brought me out of it was my parents telling me that I could major in art at college instead of taking a business course. I felt like a prisoner released from a cell, it was such wonderful news that the physical handicap became a small thing. I felt I could stand just about anything if I could have a career in art. It was the end of my depression.

* * * *

My engagement was the turning point of my life. I had always felt that I was an unattractive girl. I had inferiority feelings so bad that I once saw a psychiatrist after I had had some suicidal thoughts. For most girls I suppose engagement means home and children, independenc and the status of being married. For me these were all less important than being loved enough for marriage by a man I greatly admired. Nothing ever raised my confidence so much. My mother once said that a woman could stand anything if she is sure that she is loved, and I believe this is true. From that time on I felt much stronger as a person and actually more confident in other things; I mean things that had nothing to do with marriage.

An absorbing interest may become linked with a larger dimension of existence through meanings discovered in it or "read" into it, and which may arouse a "religious" kind of dedication. A young college teacher with a career in nuclear physics acknowledged the loneliness of agnosticism, but felt that his work brought him close to the core of cosmic events and meanings—to the "very roots of reality." "Apart from this, the fascination of the work itself is enough to fill my life without much need of anything else. I guess you could call it my religion, but it is more like a great adventure." *

Albert Einstein, writing of the piety of his youth, interpreted this "religious paradise" as his first attempt to free himself from an ego-centered ("merely personal") existence. He later became aware of the physical world as a "great eternal riddle" awaiting study and promising release from self. He noticed that "many a man whom I had learned to esteem and admire had found *inner freedom and security* in devoted occupation with it. . . . Similarly motivated men of the present and of the past, as well as the insights which they had achieved, were the friends

* "It not infrequently occurs that the scientist finds more existential meaning in his search for truth than does the religionist in his faith (hence the rise in some quarters of 'scientism,' scientific method elevated to the level of religious faith or ultimate concern)." Havens, J. In Havens, J. (ed.), *Psychology and Religion.* Princeton, N.J.: D. Van Nostrand Company, Inc., 1968, p. 23.

which could not be lost. The road to this paradise was not as comfortable and alluring as the road to the religious paradise; but it has proved itself as trustworthy, and I have never regretted having chosen it." [32]

The statement testifies that such dedication may in part serve the religious need. The "similarly motivated men" with whom he could feel linked in a bond of mutual absorption in science were a source of emotional security. A closely similar observation was made by Vincent van Gogh, who in his loneliness often gained support from the thought that other artists, perhaps unknown to him, were also seeking a meaningful existence through devotion to creative work.

In some biographical studies the writer once suggested that:

the luckiest people on earth are the "great obsessionals," meaning not the neurotic variety but those so passionately devoted to an interest or a cause and so little deflected by the urges that move others toward money and acclaim, or even toward food, rest, and sleep, that their behavior is very noticeably unlike that of their fellows . . . not only are these fortunate creatures never bored except when they are forced to be inactive, and rarely uncertain in their decisions as to what they want to do. They are mainly enviable because the obsessional pursuit is endlessly full of zest and fascination, and because they so often manage to make it of unquestionably high significance in the scale of human values. [35, 36]

The literature of biography is rich in evidence that zestful and absorbing lives are possible without religious foundation, and that the truth that religion gives meaning to life does not exclude the truth that vitally fulfilling meanings may have other sources.

"All our affections," writes Bertrand Russell, "are at the

mercy of death, which may strike down those whom we love at any moment. It is therefore necessary that our lives should not have that narrow intensity which puts the whole meaning and purpose . . . at the mercy of accident." [75] Reactions to stress are often intensified in persons with narrowly limited interests and personal attachments. A vital factor in tolerance for stress lies in the number and strength of emotional investments in a variety of living areas. "Diversification," as applied in economics, may be useful in the emotional sphere and for the same reasons. One is less likely to be shaken by events and harried by anxieties when living patterns are built around emotion-centering interests.

In an age when so many are engaged in sterile routines in which opportunity for personal expression is rarely possible, exhortations toward interest development as a way of restoring meaningfulness and of lifting morale may appear to be ironic. One of the movements in modern philosophy is centered, on the other hand, with just such needs. Here the focus is less on cosmic issues and generalities than upon the personal meanings of experience. "There are some philosophers who are far more interested in human realities, or in helping people to cure themselves of spiritual maladies . . . than they are in constructing [a] . . . philosophy of nature." [37] Among their concerns are the questions illustrated in the early chapters of this book: the anxieties, depressions, apathy and despair caused by events which bring the basic issues of living into the foreground. Again the importance of individuality emerges, since the meaningfulness of any major activity depends so greatly on temperament and inclination. Here the natural ethics of evolution, the historical movement toward freedom and the guideline of "each to his own" converge in their bearing on the issues of personal fulfillment. The quest has a long background, from Socrates' effort to teach a student "to give birth to his own new personality by having him know himself more lucidly" to Nietzsche's exhortation: "Be yourself! What you are at present doing, opining, and desiring, that is not really you." [71]

*   *   *

A large question remains: In the absence of sustaining nonreligious motivation is a life of adequate fulfillment possible without religious belief of some kind or degree? Is evidence of purposiveness in evolution and of progress in the historical record enough, or must there be, in addition, something of traditional "faith, hope and promise" to make existence bearable, acceptable or even enjoyable? A student of individuality would probably answer—and would surely be right—that for some it is possible and for others it may not be.

Such a finding would at least prove that the religious need is not "instinctive." While religious beliefs do not influence people uniformly, one might expect, in their absence, some signs of spiritual malaise if the need were a universal of human psychology. In Western society there have been, in every age and century, those who have lived serene and productive lives without benefit of supernatural certainties. With regard to morality it has often been said: "Within the fold of organized religion bigots and brutes exist, while outside the fold are many considerate, selfless men." [10] Within the fold there have also been many who have been distraught and insecure about the fundamentals, and many outside it who have achieved tranquillity regarding the basic issues. Either through personal philosophies, devotion to secular pursuits or other resources they have successfully solved the existential problem.

More convincing, however, would be a great civilization

not only free, relatively, of emotional dependence on the supernatural, but without evidence that this freedom had crippled its capacity to sustain itself, to develop a high level of culture and to find adequate rewards in an earthbound philosophy.

In preface to an effort to answer the question, a brief reference to the body of thought known as "humanism" will be helpful. Of the several meanings of the term, one is of special interest here.*

Its main focus is upon man, his place in the natural world and the quality of his life. Humanists may affirm, deny or leave open the issue of what may lie beyond life as we know it, but they agree that man's best hope must rest on the high probability that all he will ever have on earth will depend on his own efforts. The wisest course, therefore, is for him to live *as if* the world he has is all there is, and that the natural span of years is all he can be sure of. As one humanist puts it: the possibility of the supernatural is not denied; it is only dismissed; it is not needed.

The foremost and essential faith and confidence is in human powers and potentialities. What man has accomplished is rich evidence of what he can do. Humanism relies on science as a means of unlimited improvement of

---

* The varieties of humanism differ mainly in emphasis. Most of the outline here is taken from the publications of the journal *The Humanist* (Yellow Springs, Ohio: The American Humanist Association) and from the "Humanist Manifesto." [55] The essentials include faith in human capacity and potential and in scientific method applied to human relationships. Ethical values are to be formulated on naturalistic premises (as versus supernatural sources). The movement is democratic and antinationalist; it proclaims the basic kinship of all men. Unlimited progress is achievable through cooperative conquest of every human problem. Everything supportive of human endeavor—all "help"—must come, not from outside the natural order but from human competence and willingness to respond to the needs of others.

the human condition. "Salvation" and security lie in our ability to apply it to all human relationships, individual, national and international.

Humanist ethics are earth centered and based on human values. Tolerance, respect for different points of view, freedom within the limits that safeguard individual rights, are primary. Moral behavior is a means to earthly well-being rather than to supernatural rewards. The highest ideal is service to others. Humanism "insists on the reality of genuine altruism as one of the moving forces in the affairs of men . . . it reaffirms the spirit of cosmopolitanism, of international friendship, and of the essential brotherhood of man. Humanists feel *compassionate concern* for their fellowmen throughout the globe." [56]

A traditional religious premise for the doctrine of human equality is that in spirit or "soul" all men are the same despite the many differences in ability, energy and other traits. They are equal in value "in the sight of God." The approach of humanism would be closer to the view that men are mainly equal or alike in that all want satisfactions of similar kinds, that all want contentment, freedom from frustration, distress and anxiety. The difference between the highest and lowest levels of abilities is enormous, but there is no comparable evidence that experiences of fear and anger, joy and sorrow, differ to the same degree. Such experiences may not be identical from person to person but men are far more similar in these ways than in overall capacities.

The humanist tends to feel that if life is lived to its fullest there will or need be small concern as to what, if anything, lies beyond it. If all its potentials are fulfilled, there may be little desire left. A philosopher writes: "The life I want is a life I could not endure in eternity. It is a life of love and intensity, suffering and creation, that makes life worth while and death welcome. . . . As one deserves a good night's sleep, one also deserves to die." [54] The humanist believes that a richly rewarding and purposeful life is possible without hope of a further extension. He believes also that there is nobility in living to the fulfillment of a purpose and courage in living a commitment without hope of a reward beyond it.*

Humanism, in sum, is naturalistic, as versus supernaturalistic; ethical; and humanitarian. It is democratic, optimistic, confident of man's capacity to solve all earthly problems. It believes that life as we know it offers resources and possibilities that can enrich our lives so greatly that the promises of religion may for many be no longer needed.

The humanist movement is large and active, comprising many groups, and persons of eminence and influence. It is widely regarded as adapted to some basic features of American society and traditions.

The religions most familiar to peoples of the Western world are centered on the relationship between man and

* Much contemporary unbelief, writes a member of a conference on the meaning of the death of God, is not so much a rebellious reaction as "a quiet indifference which develops in people who discover that they can be complete human beings without religious faith . . . they come to realize that work, knowledge, art . . . are worthwhile in themselves, and that one can fill his life with them so that the Church, and even God, becomes unnecessary." [1]

A theologian sums up an aspect of the "death of God" movement in historical perspective:

God has been steadily losing ground and man has been steadily gaining ground as man finds ways of solving more and more of his problems, of satisfying more and more of his needs, without appealing to God for help. The further back into the past we look, the more helpless man appears to have been in the face of life and the basic problems of life, such as hunger, sickness, warfare and death. The further into the future we project this same line of development, the more we can expect man to have solved these problems and to have become capable of helping himself. [25]

God; on moral behavior; on "salvation" and what is necessary for it. They regard earthly existence as headed toward an infinite future with rewards and punishments, and there is much emphasis on worship and prayer.[33]

In wide contrast is an example from the Far Eastern cultures. China has long been preeminently "the home of humanistic, or non-theological, philosophy." This oldest of living societies, with a tradition dating back almost four thousand years, has managed to achieve high cultural levels in the relative absence of the religious supernaturalism which many regard as essential, suggesting that man does not require support of this kind in order to live with wisdom and serenity. "The Chinese never dedicated themselves to the service of God, in love or in fear. . . . Their civilization was humanistic through and through. Its spiritual values were purely human values, unclouded by other-worldliness or notions of pure spirituality. Its highest goals were natural goods, good for this life and good enough without the further promise of an eternal life." [65]

The Chinese humanists believe they have found the true end of life . . . the end of life lies not in life after death, for the idea that we live in order to die, as taught by Christianity, is incomprehensible; nor in nirvana, for that is too metaphysical; nor in the satisfaction of accomplishment, for that is too vainglorious; nor yet in progress for progress' sake, for that is meaningless. The true end, the Chinese have decided in a singularly clear manner, lies in the enjoyment of a simple life, especially the family life, and in harmonious social relationships . . .

The difference between China and the West seems to be that the Westerners have a greater capacity for getting and making more things and a lesser ability to enjoy them, while the Chinese have a greater determination and capacity to enjoy the few things they have. This trait, our concentration on earthly happiness, is as much a result as a cause of the absence of religion. For if one cannot believe in the life hereafter as the consummation of the present life, one is forced to make the most of this life. . . . The absence of religion makes this concentration possible.[57]

Among the traditions of our society is the belief that morality must have the support of religion. Man's impulses would otherwise run wild, it is assumed, and make social order impossible to maintain. Only a "god-fearing" man is morally reliable. Without heavenly hopes and fears, men would not endure the restraints that make group living possible. In primitive societies religious taboos have sometimes had the force of laws. Myths involving the supernatural may give authority to codes concerning desirable behavior.

Many exceptions to this linkage of morals with religion appear in the history of cultures. That of China has demonstrated "the most effective morality to be found among the peoples of any time; a social organization that has held together more human beings, and has endured through more centuries, than any other known to history."[26] Confucius, five centuries before Christ and without the help of supernatural sanctions, made the golden rule a fundamental of conduct. The highest ideals in human relationships, he taught, were tolerance, sympathy, compassion and fellowship feeling.

Much of the history of China, as often said, is that of the influence of Confucius. His chief concern was practical morality. All or most of his maxims are familiar homilies on virtues in personal relationships. Among them are sincerity and naturalness; courtesy, generosity, and justice; respect for others and willingness to consider their points of view; willingness to acknowledge errors. "Confucius was asked, 'Is there one word that sums up the basis of all god conduct?' and he replied, 'Is not "reciprocity" that word? What you yourself do not desire, do not put before others.' " [34] He had much to say about the importance of the family in its role in the development of character. The moral man is not the pious devotee of things divine but the mature personality, wise in all the ways that make for insightful treatment of others and serenity in everyday life.*

Confucius has been classed as agnostic owing to his negative or indifferent attitude toward theological matters. While the Chinese have had a theology, it was not the same for the educated classes as for the masses of the people. For the former, deity was an impersonal symbol of the moral order of the universe and of society; for the latter it was more personalized. Religion, for the peasant, meant the worship of ancestral spirits and a variety of good and evil minor entities, some dating from the nature gods of antiquity. † [27]

The Chinese may therefore be said to have a religion, but their theology included no certitudes concerning "the origin, destiny, or ultimate meaning of the universe." Like the Greeks and Romans, they "managed decently and graciously enough without expecting God to consummate their history. . . . The Chinese were content to leave the

* "Concerning the spirits and their action among men," writes an historian, Confucius "was always reticent. There is no reason to suppose that he doubted their existence or their power; but he systematically refused to discuss theological or metaphysical questions. . . . The world of men and morals came first; speculation about Heaven or the nature of life after death he simply put aside." [58]

† "China is agnostic and scarcely knows a religion in the Western sense. . . . While the Chinese mind is earthbound, it is strongly drawn to magic. It sees the world inhabited by a multitude of spirits. . . . The aggregate of thousands of such superstitions is not transcendental or spiritual. It is not an attempt to commune with the unseen forces but to constrain them . . ." [81]

unknowable alone." [66] The idea of earthly existence as but a preparation, or of virtue as a bid for future rewards rather than as the basis of a happier world, has always been alien to them. The Chinese citizen has long been "the most secular spirit . . . in known history; *this* life absorbs him; and when he prays he asks not for happiness in paradise, but for some profit here on earth." [28]

What has been the quality of life of a people whose philosophy has been so different from our own? In many ways the history runs parallel to that of most others, including that of Western societies: poverty and strife, corruption and oppression, misgovernment and civil wars. The masses of the peasantry, as in other lands, were victimized by taxation, periodically devastated by drought, flood and famine. Despite the refined ideals of Confucianism among the upper classes the religion of the peasantry has been a complex of crude superstitions. Nor have the Chinese been free of selfishness and stupidity, brutality and callousness. The overall record, in brief, is as depressing in many respects as that of Christian Europe.

It is equally clear, however, that this history is not to be seen as the product of humanism, that the failures cannot be charged against an earthbound philosophy. Chinese orientation toward material change, or "progress," has been widely different from that of the West. Their reaction to nature has tended to be esthetic. They have not been interested in understanding its movements and processes. In consequence they did not until recently make notable progress in either science or technology. For lack of the impulse for scientific inquiry they were for centuries deprived of the fruits of research which have been basic to the advances of the West.

The teachings of Confucius, despite their value for social ethics, have had a marked negative side. The master gave great weight to the "wisdom of the ancients," and Chinese society continued his conservative posture in emphasis on conformity and acceptance. The world was respected as inherently good; the idea that the conditions of life could be changed was foreign to their thought habits. "Assuming that it was a moral order, which in the long run always rewarded virtue with success, they put up with a great deal of misrule, resisting efforts at reform as interferences with the natural order." [67] Among other factors the cult of ancestor worship was hardly a stimulus to originality or to an open attitude toward the development of the individual.

Thus a great people with impressive achievements in the specialized arts as well as in the arts of living did more than survive four thousand years without the kind of religious supports regarded as vital to morale in Western cultures. During their Golden Ages, at least, "the Chinese represented without doubt the highest civilization and the ripest culture that Asia, or perhaps any continent, had yet achieved." [29] The great advances in the material conditions of life made by Western science, on the other hand, and as historians have often observed, were not only independent of religious orientation but were often in conflict with it.

*   *   *

For some an example of humanistic society taken from the "oriental mind" may seem too alien to have impressive weight. Chinese culture may be thought so unlike ours in racial temperament as to make a weak defense for this philosophy and world view.

A further instance, much "closer to home," is available in a Western society which, though ancient, has long been recognized as the source of certain features of our own, and as outstanding in the history of freedom and creativity.

The classical Greeks, like the Chinese, had a religion, but again in a greatly different sense from those of the West and the Near East. It has been called a human-centered rather than a god-centered religion in that the many gods of the Greeks were the most humanlike of any of the major religions. The inhabitants of Olympus were by our standards hardly divinities at all, being little more than projections of man himself in all his limitations and shortcomings, moral and otherwise. They offered no account of the origin and purpose of the universe and could not easily have been though of as omnipotent and benevolent. Though more than human in powers, they were never much more than glorified human beings in other ways.

In Homer, the "Bible of the Greeks," man, not the gods, is the main actor. The Greeks looked to great men for their ideals rather than to their divinities. They recognized human vices and follies, but the gods inspired no sense of guilt; "they lived neither in fear nor in love of God but went about their own business of making the most of life on earth." [69]

While religion played an important part in Greek life it meant for the individual not so much doctrinal faith as formal practices; "there was no church, no orthodoxy, no rigid creed." There were outstanding skeptics among them who anticipated modern humanism. One of them (Protagoras) is quoted: "With regard to the gods I know not whether they exist or not, or what they are like. Many things prevent our knowing: the subject is obscure, and brief is the span of our mortal life." [30]

On the whole Greek religion was far more secular, worldly and earthbound, "nonreligious," than our own. It was a product, not of prophets and holy men, but of poets and philosophers.[38] Greek morale was sustained by confidence in man's own powers and his capacity for excellence rather than by convictions about the supernatural. "Greeks in general thought only vaguely about life after death, and most men seemed doubtful that any existed."[15] Man as an individual was of supreme importance, and this was itself a novelty, since the concept of "the entire unimportance of the individual to the state . . . was universally accepted in all the ancient world." [39] Respect for the person is reflected in the fact that it was a Greek (Euripides) who was first to condemn the institution of human slavery, accepted without question throughout the ancient world, and even by the Old Testament prophets; "to the Greek, human beings were not chiefly different but chiefly alike." [40]

The outstanding symbol of the Greek spirit—as was Confucius of the Chinese—was Socrates. Agnostic regarding the Gods, he "advised his followers not to dispute of such matters; like Confucius, he asked them did they know human affairs so well that they were ready to meddle with those of heaven." [31] He did not offer to interpret the divine purposes and was uncertain of life after death, but he was greatly concerned about wisdom and justice on earth, about rational morality and a better life founded on reason. The highest good was to be defined as what is "good for something in this life . . . good that all men could achieve by their own efforts. . . . He sought wisdom rather than holiness, sanity rather than sanctity." [70] This was a clear statement of the philosophy of humanism, twenty-four hundred years ago, and one of the products of "the most creatively precious culture that history records."

*   *   *

A letter from a correspondent, a professional counselor and a student of philosophy who read this book in manuscript is included here as a partial summary, and because a few pertinent questions are raised.

The issues illustrated in your case studies are, as you know, nothing novel in philosophic literature, though presented in unusually concrete and personalized form.

With regard to the discussion of man as a natural predator it might have been added that he has been not only an aggressor against his own kind but a carnivorous one as well in view of the large amount of archeological evidence of cannibalism in many parts of the world. We take completely for granted, incidentally, the assembly-line slaughter of millions of animals every year. Each morsel of flesh we eat is as much a symbol of the predator as the killing of a deer by a lion (that jolted one of your subjects into a new perception of "natural evil").

A distinction between two different kinds of evil may need emphasis. People tend to think of floods, earthquakes, disease and deformity as somehow reconcilable with the traditional image of deity. They are "accidents," or perhaps "intended" to stimulate character growth through ordeal, or to test faith, etc. Since they are occasional they may be regarded as exceptional and thus not a part of the normal course of existence. But exploitation in nature cannot be seen in this way, being neither occasional nor accidental. It is part, as you indicate, of the basic structure. It makes a different problem from such assumedly man-made evils as crime, alcoholism, drug addiction and other ills regarded as resulting from human weakness, willfulness, perversity, etc.

The discussion of evolution raises large questions about orthodox theory but the possibility remains that more research will dispose of some of them. The recent great advances in genetics and those sure to follow may provide some answers. It's the old "God of the gaps" argument, bringing in deity or the supernatural wherever knowledge is lacking. As it increases, the weight of evidence regarding "design and purpose" may be altered.

The matter of direction and progress in history reduces finally, as your treatment shows, to the basic ethical issue. Enormous advance in technology is of course beyond question, and even great moral progress, in the very long run, and despite the horrors of the present century. Yet continued advance of every kind, even to Utopia, would simply intensify the greatest issue of all: the sacrifice of the billions of poor wretches of the past who paid for Utopia with their efforts.

This leads, however, not to the "new supernaturalism" (the old theology), but to a new and much revised concept of deity. The scientific theologians offer us a God who really did make the best of all possible worlds—meaning the best he could do, despite the glaring imperfections. But can we accept such an entity as *God*? Why not just the Manichean dualism of good and evil forces, and the simple deduction that we must struggle against the one and try to advance the other?

Your Case #4 (Chapter 1) raises the question of development in the personality as a concrete case of the issue of purposiveness in the vastly larger dimension of evolution as a whole. Some kind of growth in the individual seems a valid test of the entire concept of purpose. But how about Nietzsche's statement that the lives of the great masses of mankind are no more significant ("purposive"?) than those of the lower animals; that the difference between one man and another may be far greater than that between many men and the lower animals? How do we "keep the faith" if the greater part of humanity is expendable?

A natural theology must certainly include the vast range of individual differences, since it is inseparable from the enormous disparities in the quality of lives—the differences in achievement, in happiness, frustration and misery. These differences between the fortunates and the unfortunates (no fault) which ethically—not biologically—considered seem infinitely *wrong*, make a foremost challenge for anyone trying to justify deity.

Your psychological approach to the religious problem is, I gather, mainly a social-emotional one, since discussion of the rational philosophies is brief. To have absorbing interests and strong bonds with others appears to be the essence of it. Fully occupied people do not seem much concerned about religious issues, which are much more likely to be of interest to the lonely, the failed, or bored. Goethe would probably have agreed with this, since he once said (*Conversations with Ecker-mann*) with reference to immortality, that people who haven't much to do are likely to dwell on it, but that "an able man, who has something regular to do here, and must toil and struggle and produce day by day, leaves the future world to itself, and is active and useful in this one."

It would be of interest to know how large a part of the population becomes genuinely concerned about existential matters at any time in the course of life.

With regard to evolution my correspondent points to the possible effect of increasing knowledge on its interpretation. The direction of such developments cannot, however, be foreseen. They may confirm and further reveal internal directedness and purposiveness. Some problems become even greater as knowledge increases, as in the case of the quantum phenomenon in physics, where the nature of energy has ceased to be imaginable and can only be represented by abstract symbols. Among the professionals whose views have been summarized there are clear statements that the behavior of organisms cannot conceivably be understood as products of chance plus selection. No more can the mathematically precise movements of the planets.*

As to the image of deity which appears to follow from the findings reviewed the question is asked: Why not accept that there are good and evil forces or agencies and

---

* "In the evolution of scientific thought one fact has become impressively clear: there is no mystery of the physical world which does not point to a mystery beyond itself. . . . All highroads of the intellect, all byways of theory and conjecture, lead ultimately to an abyss that human ingenuity can never span." * "However far our gaze penetrates," Whitehead has written, "there are always heights beyond that block our vision." * Barnett, L. *The Universe and Dr. Einstein.* New York: New American Library, Inc., 1960, p. 117. Whitehead, A. N. *Process and Reality.* New York: The Macmillan Company, 1929.

content ourselves with aiding the ones and overcoming the others? Why personify the dualism?

Theologians of nature have seen grounds for doing both. There is the supreme fact of creativity at work in evolution. Out of it has come the highest products of human achievement as well as the ethical conflict. The latter has emerged as the direction and character of purposiveness itself appears to have changed.

Creation by trial and error is a *method*, and any method is more than chaos. The thought has been expressed in many ways. "If nature has produced man . . . then it would seem that man gives some indication of the nature of nature. . . . The creative processes of the universe have produced self-conscious beings with a degree of intelligence and a drive to search for truth, beauty, and goodness. Is it reasonable to believe that a process devoid of purpose and intelligence could produce a being like man?" [82]

Natural theology offers an image of an agency "motivated" to create (otherwise "Why not nothing?"). It is limited to a groping, uncertain and vastly time-needing method, but achieves enormous and progressive change of well-defined character. It has passed from an amoral to a moral phase, with resulting disharmony and stress. This is far from the traditional idea of what a God must be, but some have found it nearer to the realities.

My correspondent raises the question of growth in the individual life course, as a "test" of purposiveness in evolution, and refers to the Nietzschean doctrine that the masses of mankind are without significance, that only the creative elite have meaning in the cosmic frame. Granted the biological and psychological evidence which seems to support this thesis, the ethical reaction, the "cry for justice" against the inequalities, is as much a part of nature as the evils that have raised it. In the cosmic as well as in the human sense

—if the distinction can be made—they are not acceptable, leaving the issue to be resolved in the theologies earlier outlined. If we are not reconciled, we are not "alone" in our revolt, which is rooted in the core of what deity has given us.

It is true that the psychological approach offered here is mainly social-emotional, and that there is small discussion of rational solutions. The humanist position may include both, however, and examples have been given. Religious interpretations are not excluded, but remain as background possibilities. *Meanwhile* we can work wholeheartedly with what we can be sure of: that we are seemingly left to our own resources of self-help and mutual aid. There remains the ancient logic that if life as we know it is truly all there is, we will have done our best to make it worthwhile, and if there is more, we have lost nothing and shall have made gains regardless of what is further in store for us.

The final question deserves a more extended comment. "One of the wonders of life," someone has said, "is that so few have wondered about it." The best minds have probed and pondered its meaning for centuries, but one would never suspect this from observations of the daily lives of the vast majority, most of whom take it as much for granted as do the lower animals. There are needs to be satisfied, demands to be met and threats to be avoided. Living patterns become deeply habitual. As awareness grows with maturity, the larger dimensions of the world's activities become increasingly defined, but basic questions are rarely raised. The goals our culture has established as rewarding and generally approved are adopted with little query.

For an hour or two a week, perhaps, the mind of the church goer may pause to dwell upon the overall meaning, but here again the established doctrines are seldom challenged. Realities which appear to clash with them may at times be perturbing, but such uneasiness does not often persist. The persons whose mental and emotional distresses provided an introduction to the themes of this book are hardly valid samples of the members of our society, though the fact that their numbers are increasing was the motive for its writing.

Ours is not an introspective culture. If we unthinkingly accept existence without question it is, in part, because we are surrounded by others who would react with wonder, puzzlement or impatience if the question were raised. The daily routines, far from stimulating such a query, are a fairly continuous distraction from it. When we do become contemplative our thoughts are outwardly directed; if we think about ourselves it is in relation to external events. A culture more inwardly turned (as that of India, for example) impresses us as alien and peculiar.

There is no novelty in such observations, nor in speculation on the sources of our bias toward this kind of worldliness and away from matters more subjective. The high place of science, with its focus on the physical world, has played a part. The historic role of the frontier tradition with its demands upon extroverted living has been a factor through its preoccupation with material achievement rather than with personal growth. The Protestant "ethic of work" may be another.

A reaction has set in, especially during the last quarter century, against this imbalance in the mental set of our living pattern. It includes, with much else, rejection of the tendency toward mass uniformity and loss of the value of individuality. It rebels against the concept of man as an object to be manipulated as has been done so successfully with physical nature (symbolized by such phrases as "human engineering," as if people were functional units to be controlled). It would regard every man as a personal entity to be respected, at least, if not reverenced as an embodiment of some part of evolutionary purpose.

Such a movement is in harmony with every effort toward individual orientation in religion. "Whatever the fate of institutional religion may be," writes Gordon Allport, "the subjective . . . religious sentiments of mankind . . . are very much alive and will perhaps always remain alive, for their roots are many and deep." From childhood on individuality demands expression. "Our organisms are so constructed that our personal life is the highest value that we ever know directly." Allport has marked, more than any other modern student of religious psychology, the variety of ways in which individuality may be achieved in this area. In an age of insecurity and alienation, when religion itself is "the most doubt-ridden, the most elusive of all the fields of mental activity," one who has lost the moorings of orthodoxy is increasingly on his own resources in resolving the basic issues.

Man's exploratory urge, which led to science; the gift that enabled him to build culture; the insight that gave him his sense of justice; the compassion and the revolt against suffering and cruelty that have aroused his central conflicts—all had their origins in the processes that molded him into what he has become. Organic evolution made him; he does not "make himself," nor ever did. The tradition that he reflects the image of deity can only mean that the creative source must share in the stresses which are at root its own.

If, as biologists have assured us, we are still evolving, the purposiveness inherent in evolution will continue active within us, and whatever we find ourselves striving to achieve will express a Will infinitely greater than our own. In harmony with such a premise we may continue to act in essential self-dependence, and consistent with the humanist doctrine that men can help themselves, that they will help each other and that no more than this is needed.

Not all, but much of what traditional religion has given may be found in a new theology and in a deepened sense of community. Faith in human capacity and response, however smaller than faith in deity, is more tangible and perhaps less insecure. The doctrinal frame may be lacking, but the emotional supports are available and are more vital by far.

Appendix Notes

Introduction

Text page 3

One of the writer's students in a course in evolutionary biology was disturbed over the evidence that man's development from the lower animals through a series of intermediate anthropoid forms (the links were *not* missing) had been *continuous*. "If the evolution was absolutely unbroken, if there was no place a line could be drawn, it would have to mean that all the lower animals, like ourselves, have 'immortal souls.'" He found this very hard to accept. "But if they don't, and if it was really continuous, then . . ." He found the alternative also hard to accept.

Chapter 1

Text page 19

An article on psychological help for religious insecurity, published by the writer in *Pastoral Psychology* (1970), elicited a number of comments, some illustrating fairly well the kind of issues of "ultimate concern" on which this book is centered.

The following example touches on one of the several outlined in Chapter 1.

I find that I cannot separate the idea of life's overall purpose from that of *development*. Somehow there has got to be mental change, growth, if there is to be meaning. The way it is for the great majority, just earning a living at some sterile routine in order to eat, have a shelter, reproduce, etc., is simply not enough.

It seems to me, when I think of the narrow, repetitive, commonplace existence of most people, that there is hardly any *evidence* of purpose in the individual life. I think of the millions of peasants, and especially of the savages, who have lived for ages almost like animals.

If there *is* purpose, it surely fails to an enormous extent; for example the millions of infants who have died at birth or soon after, and the mental defectives who stay child-like all their lives.

I read somewhere that "the rank and file of mankind are only the material of evolution, not its goal," that it is the species that matters, not the individual. Biologists seem to agree that there has been enormous *waste* in evolution. Billions of the unfit were eliminated. Many species became extinct because they failed to change in certain ways. Always it was just the few who were "selected" to survive.

It has struck me like a blow that the same could be true of the so-called "anonymous masses" of human beings, that most of them could be *waste*, too. Maybe the whole purpose is in the exceptional few who survive. I mean who change in some important way.

This idea shocks me deeply, yet the case is strong. It is scientifically sound. If it isn't true, what the hell are people *for*?

Some would, of course, reject the equation of purpose to development, holding that any fulfillment, however limited, is an end in itself and confers meaning. Others, like Nietzsche, have regarded the "masses" as having value only as the raw potential from which the elite few are recruited, and as otherwise outside the concept of life as a creative process.

Text page 39

Below is an excerpt from one of a number of examples. The subject is a businessman; mid-fifties; Protestant.

Recently I counted the number of church advertisements in the newspaper announcing Sunday services and found that 14 out of 18 included the word "worship," usually implying that the service itself was in essence a worship.

When I think of all the world's ills and the miseries that people can't possibly have brought on themselves (for example, the famines in India and China), the diseases, floods and other disasters, I just can't accept the idea of worship. It makes me think of a dog licking the hand of its master after being beaten for something it couldn't help. To tell the truth, the word simply makes me sick when I think of some of the things I've seen or heard about. Indignation, yes; even anger, and certainly *question*, but worship, no.

I once discussed this with the minister of our church. He was a bit evasive about things like diseases and famines. He put the emphasis on what he called "man s responsibility." His main point was that when God gave man freedom to act He could not be "held" for what was done with the freedom. He went on to say what a wonderful thing freedom was, and that life would not be worth living without it. He said that next to life itself this was God's greatest gift to man and reason enough for us to worship him, even without all the other wonderful things in the world.

All I could say was that we are taught that God is "our Father," and that we are all "children of God," and that if I gave complete freedom to a child, knowing that it *might* injure itself seriously, I would feel not only responsible but guilty if it did, and I would not expect the child to be grateful for the gift, let alone worship me for it.

The main religious problem for me is not whether God exists but what *kind* of a God he must be in order to make sense out of the way things are in the world. I don't see how you can have faith unless your idea of God helps to do that.

Chapter 2

Text page 55

Dobzhansky has written: "Evolution is a creative process in precisely the same sense in which composing a poem or a symphony, carving a statue, or painting a picture are creative acts." [9] The comparison may be questioned when related to his own view of evolution as selection from chance mutations. An artist selects from his materials the elements that express his purpose until the original intention is achieved, but it cannot be said that he proceeds by wholly undirected moves toward his goal. His actions are guided by the image that symbolizes his purpose. The image may be said to select, but what it selects *from* are not blindly random acts, as would be assumed if natural selection is to be illustrated in terms of artistic creation.

There is, it is true, a school of art which appears to proceed by the chance-and-selection method, but its productions are probably not what Dobzhansky had in mind.

Text page 57

A biologist states: "There is no scintilla of scientific proof that evolution in the sense of progression from less to more complicated organisms had anything to do with better adaptation, selective advantage or production of larger offspring. Adaptation is possible at any level of organization. An ameba, a worm, an insect . . . are well adapted . . . if they were not, they would have become extinct long ago." *

Another writes that many students of the problem agree that the increasing complexity of organisms is a major issue of evolutionary theory and acknowledges the possibility "that there is a non-random feature, perhaps at the very basis of the natural order . . ." †

Text page 58

After suggesting that hunger for the "unfathomable and the infinite" is a biologically determined human trait, Dobzhansky concedes that it has no apparent adaptive value, but has survived as part of the complex which includes the capacity for language and abstract thought.

Since he regards it as unfavorable to adaptation the question

---

* Bertalanffy, L. von. In Koestler, A., and Smythies, J. R. (eds.). *Beyond Reductionism: New Perspectives in the Life Sciences* (The Alpbach Symposium 1968). New York: The Macmillan Company, 1969, p. 67.
† Thorpe, W. H. In *op. cit.*, p. 432.

remains why it has not been eliminated by the same process whereby, as with camouflage or mimicry, even extremely minute departures from pattern are assumed to be deleted.

It has also been questioned whether abstract thought is essentially related to the "metaphysical hunger," since the former is quite conceivable without the latter.

Text page 65

G. G. Simpson writes that while "purpose and plan are not characteristic of evolution and not a key to any of its operations," both must have entered the process with man, since he "has purposes and . . . makes plans." The basic cause must therefore lie in man himself; the purposes and plans "are ours, not those of the universe." [34]

This seems to imply that we have, as purposive beings, somehow created this component of our own makeup. We are told that man, who is unique, developed out of a "new organization" of the materials of evolution. The question remains how a purposive creature evolved out of purposeless antecedents. Unless it can be answered it seems permissible to believe that purpose was present from the beginning.

Chapter 3

Text page 74

A student of universal history suggests that the only "theology" supported by the total of human experience is that of a struggle between good and evil forces, a conclusion in harmony with much modern scientific philosophy and with the findings on ethics reviewed in Chapter 3. "There is glaring conflict," writes a biologist, "between the 'gladiatorial theory of existence,' seemingly implied in the evolutionary theory, and the Golden Rule, which . . . still stands as the most comprehensive statement of the guiding principle of ethics." [14]

Something akin to compassion began with the response of the maternal animal to the needs of offspring. A new phase dawned with sympathetic response to others extending beyond the limits of the family circle. A student of the origins of morality writes: "The surviving documents demonstrate . . . that the 'moral consciousness of mankind' has grown up with each generation out of the . . . emotions of family life. . . . The supreme values were not anywhere upon our globe until the life of father, mother, and children created them." [5] Even among the lower animals, writes another, "we see a foreshadowing of the fact that moral qualities begin with family relationships . . ." [20] A student of the lower organisms notes that their social organization "shows so many aspects found in family life . . . it is . . . probable that in many species group life is nothing but an extension of family life." [36]

Compassion, then, is as deeply rooted in the natural order as the anguish of the "sacrificial" animal under the teeth of the predator, and this emotional and ethical dualism must be included in any theology willing to face nature's realities.

That these clash with related doctrines of traditional religion is starkly clear. "The human mind is profoundly dissatisfied with any form of absolute dualism, with a religion . . . for which ultimate Reality is not one and undivided." Efforts to dispose of the dualism and to preserve the omnipotence, benevolence and unity of deity lead at times to curious maneuvers. One recent apologist (Alan Watts) concedes that "man is involved in a dualistic relationship with evil" but denies that evil is incompatible with infinite divine love and power. Theology "can never admit that God is responsible for evil." It is in granting freedom to man that God permits its existence. This permission only proves his love and holiness, according to Watts, who finds no moral conflict between the concept of evil and that of divine unity. Evil "struggles against God," but fails "because he always embraces it in his all-inclusive love." A note of logic-under-strain is at times suggested in such efforts to salvage cosmic unity; e.g., the greater the evil "the greater it proves the love of God to be, because that love simply 'enlarges' itself to include and embrace it." *

* Watts, A. *Behold the Spirit: A Study in the Necessity of Mystical Religion.* New York: Random House, Inc. (Vintage Books), 1972, pp. 129, 148, 149.

Chapter 4

Text page 95

Christopher Dawson has been prominent in emphasis on the "mysterious and unpredictable aspect of history which is the great stumbling block to the rationalist." His favorite illustration is the totally unexpected development of Christianity. "What contemporary observer could have imagined that the execution of an obscure Jewish leader in the first century of the Roman Empire would affect the lives and thoughts of millions who never heard the name of the great statesmen and generals of the age?" That a "barbarous Semitic tribe" could have led to an enormous ethical revolution can only mean that hidden "spiritual" forces were at work.

"No age," he thinks, "has ever been able to foresee the age to come." The Roman world "with its power and wealth and culture and corruption sank into blood and ruin . . . but the other world, the world of apostles and martyrs . . . survived the downfall of ancient civilization and became the spiritual foundation of a new order." [15]

Text page 99

ETHICAL DUALISM IN HISTORY

A basic dualism in human history—the predatory strain versus its opposite, the compassionate acknowledgement of the rights of others—is one of the issues presented in Chapter 1, and relates to the concepts of "natural" theology outlined in Chapter 5.

The dualism is traceable throughout the historical record. The biology of the human organism has bearing on its meaning. If the mutations underlying the resultant conflicts are an expression of *oriented* evolution, the conclusion seems warranted that there has been a fundamental change of direction.

The predatory strain in human behavior has been unusually distinctive of certain peoples. One of the many examples is that of the Prussian feudal and military caste known as the

"Junkers," who contributed greatly in shaping the course of twentieth-century history by its remarkably aggressive character. The Junkers' influence upon the German nation was far greater than their numbers. From beginnings in the twelfth century these landowning Prussian aristocrats were marked by warlike qualities. There was much inbreeding; they tended to become "biological isolates."

The Junkers were remarkable "for personal bravery, warlike skill, and the ability to organize military operations." [38] They were men "who by both biological and social inheritance were warriors and looked upon war as the noblest of human occupations." It is the view of one student that while they might have become different under the influence of an entirely different tradition, they were to some degree predisposed toward traits favorable to militarism, and that background factors operated selectively to allow its full expression.

Sir Arthur Keith is among those who believe that a people with a history of strongly warlike behavior is predisposed by temperament. He concedes that if a child, "German or Mongol," were to be raised in an unwarlike society it would become a peaceful citizen, but thinks that this would mean only that the conditions which would release the predisposition would be lacking. He "cannot conceive" that a warlike pattern can persist for thousands of years if out of harmony with the innate bias of a culture. "Tradition is moulded to fit the mentality which fashions it, not the other way round." Man's nature is dual in this respect, he suggests, and the "ratio" varies from people to people.*

The impulse to victimize or dominate another is as much a root component of the human makeup as the impulse to protect and care for him. The behavior in which these impulses are expressed is *learned,* but the capacity is variable. One may find the values of his culture congenial or uncongenial to his preferences. He will accordingly learn easily or with difficulty; he will also learn with much or little interest or zest.

One is thus "born" neither a predator nor a saint, but he

---

* Keith, A. *Evolution and Ethics.* New York: G. P. Putnam's Sons, 1947.

may be inclined more to one kind of behavior than the other, just as he may be talented or untalented for learning an art or a science. A recent study makes the point with the statement that man is predisposed to learn to be aggressive because his nervous system is "wired" for such learning. "Aggression in the human species is the same as aggression in other animal species. . . . Aggression and violence occur in animal societies and do not differ in kind from their human counterpart. . . . Man added no new genetic qualities and lost no old ones in the areas of aggression and violence." [78] It is equally true that people differ in such qualities, as in every other human trait, and if individuals differ, the societies they compose will also differ in many and various ways, including the ability to learn violence.*

The same writers note that "loving behavior" as well as violence are readily learned "because we are wired to learn them; because they have both been essential to survival, and so mutation and natural selection have produced a creature which will readily learn both . . ." [76]

* * * * *

A great contrast between the Junkers and another distinctively different people completes our illustration of the dualism in basic evolutionary trends. In the sphere of religious and moral development, the ancient Hebrews, as historians have often observed, produced more outstanding leaders than any other culture. There was a strong and consistent trend toward a higher level of ethics in social relationships.

Like the Junkers they were a closely knit and interbreeding group; "anyone who married outside the Jewish fold was cut

---

* A biologist has reminded psychologists that race differences are made of the same elements as the differences among individuals, and that "if individuals within a population vary in some character . . . it is quite unlikely that the population means will be . . . the same." [21] Species and races derive from individuals, "not the other way around."

When all the evidence is in "we may find that . . . basic historical trends take many of their qualities from the innate physical and temperamental character of the people among whom they originate." [35]

off from the community." Daily life was enclosed in a variety of rules and taboos. Only the deeply devout could tolerate the tightly limited and religiously saturated living pattern; those who could not accept it withdrew. The result was "quite surely a concentration of people with strong religious ideas on the barren Judean plateau." [36]

When this tradition combined with exceptional individual ability the result was an unusual incidence of teachers and leaders. The founder of Christianity was the culmination of a long and powerful trend. A genius in the sphere of moral and religious concepts, he was one of many of only lesser stature. "A long selective process, which began with the patriarchs and reached its most strenuous development during the centuries just before Christ, seems to have been the means by which the Jews became a peculiarly religious people." [37]

Such marked differences among people have been seen by some as no more than responses to variable environmental pressures acting upon essentially identical organisms. Others regard them as rooted in the biology of emotional temperaments, perpetuated and reinforced by culture. As such they have been the origin of a dualism basic to all systems of ethics.

Chapter 5

Text page 116

Ian Barbour notes that the term "natural theology" has been used broadly for any theology not based on Biblical revelation, and more narrowly for one derived solely from nature. He suggests as a separate category those derived from religious experiences.[2]

The classical doctrine of natural religion derived from experience of the natural world, according to one student, while revealed religion is limited to special experiences associated with historical individuals, for example, the Biblical prophets.[64] He points out, however, that natural theology so defined must include religious experience itself, while revealed religion, although based on events of the past, is also mediated through human experience. Historical events, moreover, occur within a natural setting, and "do not escape the conditions of natural existence."

Text page 119

A philosopher writes:

It seems to me that when believers in God save his goodness by saying that he is not really omnipotent, they are taking the best course open to them, since both the personality and the goodness of God present much fewer difficulties if he is not conceived as omnipotent . . . it is less depressing and less revolting than the belief that the destinies of the universe are at the mercy of a being who, with the resources of omnipotence at his disposal, decided to make a universe no better than this.[51]

Text page 127

The "natural" mystical experience, that of all reality sensed or perceived as a unity, is a "widely authenticated fact. . . . In all cases the person who has the experience seems to be convinced that what he experiences . . . is . . . something far more real than what he experiences normally through his five senses. . . . It is, at its highest, a transcending of time and space in . . . an infinite mode of existence . . . in all cases . . . the impression of *reality* they leave behind is quite overwhelming. In every case—whether the experience comes unheralded or whether it is produced by drugs or Yoga techniques—the result is the same: the person . . . feels that he has gone through something of tremendous significance beside which the ordinary world of sense perception and discursive thought is almost the shadow of a shade." *

Text page 131

William James inferred from the dynamic effect of faith that "that which produces effects within another reality must be termed a reality itself." Mankind's "instinctive" belief in God produces real effects.

* Zaehner, R. C. *Mysticism: Sacred and Profane.* New York: Oxford University Press, 1971, pp. 50, 199.

The usual rejoinder to this is that no subjective experience can in itself be proof of deity, and that a belief may aid greatly in adjustment, may make people happier, yet be false. To say that the experience of subjective truth is not proof of any reality is not, however, to say that it is without meaning. Subjective experience of the divine is at least a token of a capacity rooted in the evolutionary process. Unlike other animals, man was evolved to seek meaning in existence. The experience of divinity may be seen as a product of natural selection if it gives courage, hope and confidence.

A mystic would favor the view that for those who have the experience in high degree it means capacity to *sense* (not "prove") a reality that does exist. It would be comparable to other capacities which vary greatly; thus there are mathematical truths quite beyond the grasp of the majority of mankind. Some would add telepathic and "precognitive" abilities.

Text page 140

EVOLUTIONARY PURPOSE AND INDIVIDUAL FREEDOM

One of the basic themes of this book was summarized in Chapter 5: "If . . . a creative entity is actively at work in the evolutionary process, it would seem . . . that it touches us most intimately . . . when we are deciding what we most want to become. It may be at moments when we must acutely feel our freedom that we are most closely in contact with that entity. From this it would follow that everyone is a medium, to some degree, of purposes larger than he knows."

The age-old issue of "free will" relates directly to the meaning of evolutionary purposiveness as expressed in and through willed human behavior. The position of the psychologist is, of course, that our choices, however free they may *feel*, must always have determinants, however unconscious, subtle or unknown. No further comment would be needed were it not that a prominent modern movement has proclaimed the precise opposite of this view: that certain decisions can be made with no relation to any elements of personality or circumstance —as if a pure "I" were acting in a mental vacuum, a thesis which would in effect dismiss all that has been learned over the centuries about the factors that mold behavior.

The issue has religious bearing, too, since if man is capable of an action completely *independent,* in this sense, he is not only "responsible," in an absolute sense, but is also *alone.* With this kind of freedom he moves "out of God's hands" entirely.

Such an act would be outside the realm of all causes of behavior, as if there exists a "self" detached from every source of motivation known to psychology. Rootless and without antecedents, it would be "as if it had been thrown into the mind from without . . . by a freakish demon," as one analyst puts it.[30]

The fact is that we are all subject, as Rollo May says, "to determining influences at every point. We are determined by our birth into a particular family of particular cultural and economic status, determined by our bodies, by instinctual needs, by past emotional traumas, and so on ad infinitum." [49] It is true that such factors as family, social influences and heredity may not always account for behavior, but this is largely because we do not know enough about the roots of human variability. We know too little, for example, about the effects, upon certain individuals, of features of environment common to all: the responsiveness of a Mozart to music, of a Turner to natural beauty, of a Gauss to numbers. These men could doubtless have said that they were free to choose their careers, but the choices were clearly determined by gifts which selected for them certain features of the world for exceptional interest.*

---

* Discussion here sometimes involves the question whether a person *could* in a given instance have acted otherwise than as he did. A psychologist must agree with what J. S. Mill wrote long ago:

When we think of ourselves . . . as having acted otherwise than we did, we always suppose a difference in the antecedents: we picture ourselves as having known something that we did not know, or not known something that we did know; which is a difference in the external motives; or as having desired something, or disliked something, more or less than we did; which is a difference in the internal motives . . . I therefore dispute altogether that we are conscious of being able to act in opposition to the strongest present desire or aversion.[52]

The fact that many have been impressed by the advocates of "absolute" freedom suggests a dismaying lack of grasp of the role of even well-known factors in behavior. The realms of psychology, normal and abnormal, and of genetics, are simply bypassed. Most psychologists would agree with Maslow:

Some existential philosophers are stressing the self-making of the self too exclusively. Sartre and others speak of the "self as a project," which is wholly created by the continued (and arbitrary) choices of the person himself, almost as if he could make himself into anything he decided to be . . . this is . . . directly contradicted by the facts of genetics and of constitutional psychology. As a matter of fact, it is just plain silly.[48]

A common argument for freedom is that it is essential to *responsibility*. Freedom is implied, we are told, whenever the words "ought" or "should" are used, and without it they are meaningless.

The conclusion does not follow. In many areas of behavior there are ideals and standards: to be truthful, loyal, generous, kind, etc. We are taught to strive for these goals, and we well know how far we fall short. That we "should" do something is a symbol of the ideal, or of the better choice, whatever its character. It is thus one of the controlling factors of behavior, yet is in itself without meaning unless behavior is determined, since the "ought" is intended to influence action.

According to the doctrine of freedom, failure deserves remorse, since the better course not only should but could have been followed. If, on the other hand, behavior is fully determined, one need only *regret* that he failed, and wish that his motivation toward the better course had been stronger. In review, one might say: I regret that my selfishness got the upper hand. I wish I were not this kind of person, that factors in my background had shaped me differently. I see the hurt I caused, and henceforth, through this experience, I shall try to avoid a recurrence.

A question asked by those who "believe in freedom" is:

What of moral indignation, and how are we to react to flagrant injustice, brutal cruelty and criminal behavior?

An answer may be given with a companion question: How are we to react when a child is stricken with painful disease, or when a person mentally ill injures others, or when an earthquake causes vast suffering? Indignation may also be "moral," though more abstract, when the innocent are made miserable in a variety of ways, even when the causes are impersonal. A consistent attitude toward both classes of events must be the same: regret, compassion and movement to prevent recurrence, if possible. To see the wrongdoer, for example, as an inevitable product of events and influences which have molded him into what he has become obviously does not mean that action is not to be taken. Society must be protected, but here the issue hinges on the philosophy of control. Our treatment of the wrongdoer is notoriously punitive rather than corrective. Treatment of any kind can be justified only if the intention is to modify behavior rather than to avenge injury.

* * * * *

A character in Dostoevsky's *Notes from Underground* intentionally performs a stupid act solely to prove his freedom—his revolt against being *determined* by the demands of rationality. Another character (Kirilov, in *The Possessed*) asserts that by taking his own life he proves his freedom. The argument is worth a comment.

Any person who reaches so extreme a posture has clearly ceased to be motivated by any strong emotional attachments, social bonds, or absorbing interests. The circumstances of his background and the build of his personality would determine his arrival at a point at which life holds little in promise. One does not reach so critical a station *by choice*.

Various motives could be conjectured. So great a need to assert initiative suggests severe denial in other areas. The need to achieve must have been frustrated. A supreme gesture, a great thrust of the ego, might be required to fulfill a need which the overall profile of life must have defeated. But no one chooses such an outcome; one is brought to it.

Another possibility might be defiance or perhaps a resentful aggressiveness. But this would be a reaction to experience; some kind of provocation must have occurred. No one *chooses* to make so vital a move, and obviously one does not arrive at such a position on rational grounds; one does not destroy himself to prove a point of logic. Strong feelings must be aroused, and no one, again, chooses to have such feelings—or the situation or life history which would generate them.

So Kirilov does not make his point. Only a unique circumstance and kind of person could be so greatly involved in the freedom issue. All normal motivations have ceased to matter, yet he is no more free than a person driven to the same end by despair, or by unbearable distress, or by threats he fears more than he fears the act itself, or finally by need of a *way out* that is greater than any other need. One may "self-destruct" only when all other choices have ceased to matter or have been withdrawn—but not self-canceled.*

* * * * *

In what sense, then, if any, can we be said to be free?

Man's purposiveness as expressed at the highest levels is as much a product of the evolutionary process as any other of his mental or physical structures. His creative choices are the way

---

* The case for freedom has for some been based on the fact that all mental life depends on events in the nervous system which are fundamentally physical, so that if the latter are at any level unpredictable, the corresponding mental processes must in this sense be "free."

As one of several rejoinders to this, Brand Blanshard has pointed out that although the behavior of electrons (energy fields or waves) can never be precisely known—since the operations of observing them may alter their status—this is no reason for denying that precise antecedents exist. To deny this would be "to abandon the established assumption and practice of science. Science has advanced in the past precisely because, when things happened whose causes were unknown, it was assumed that they had causes nevertheless." [14] The essential point being that antecedents must exist even though not determinable.

he *experiences* the agencies basic to the ascending complexity of animal forms.

If he is a venturesome and exploratory creature it is because this quality is inherent in him. When he fails to foresee outcomes and is at times guilty of costly errors it may be because the sources of evolutionary movement are in part blind and experimental in their courses. In his most notable spontaneities he is still the medium of underlying trends. He does not, and cannot, even in fullest self-awareness, "make himself," any more than he made the most complex organization in nature out of a single cell.

Unknown factors may introduce true novelty into behavior and new mental functions may eventually emerge out of the mutations. Man will *feel* free to express them, but he will be their medium only, not in any basic sense their creator.

Behavior is undetermined, then, only so far as the inherent purposiveness of evolution is itself undetermined. If evolution is a product of orientation combined with a free factor, then original behavior will be free in this sense, but its promptings must have genetic sources somewhere in the roots of every creative individual.

What bearing may this have on our self-image and our morale? It would seem to mean most importantly that we are not, in the deepest sense, alone. Short of faith in a hovering, responsive and solicitous deity there should be more security in close relationship with an entity vast in purpose, even if limited and uncertain, than to live abandoned to utter freedom and in the possibility of being altogether lost. To have absolute initiative would surely be a challenge to courage, but a more confident courage may come with the conviction that one's most vital promptings are rooted in an Unknown which, whatever its mysteries and shortcomings, has achieved all that is admirable in nature and in the human phenomenon.

Text page 145

"We are so much accustomed to the humanitarian outlook that we forget how little it counted in earlier ages of civilization. Ask any decent person in England or America what he thinks matters most in human conduct: five to one his answer will be 'kindness.' . . . If you had asked St. Francis what mattered in life, he would, we know, have answered 'chastity, obedience and poverty'; if you had asked Dante or Michelangelo they might have answered 'disdain of baseness and injustice'; if you had asked Goethe, he would have said 'to live in the whole and the beautiful.' But kindness, never. Our ancestors didn't use the word, and they did not greatly value the quality . . ." *

* Clark, K. *Civilisation: A Personal View.* New York: Harper & Row, Publishers, Incorporated, 1969, p. 329.

REFERENCES

Introduction

1. Allport, G. *The Individual and His Religion*. New York: The Macmillan Company, 1959, p. 75.
2. *Ibid.*, p. 69
3. Barbour, I. G. *Issues in Science and Religion*. Englewood Cliffs, N.J.: Prentice-Hall, Inc., 1966, p. 269.
4. Birch, B. C. *Nature and God*. Philadelphia: The Westminster Press, 1965, p. 10.
5. Frankl, V. E. *Man's Search for Meaning*. New York: Washington Square Press, 1963, pp. 183–84.
6. *Ibid.*
7. Jung, C. G. *Modern Man in Seach of a Soul*. London: Kegan Paul, Trench, Trubner & Co., Ltd., 1934, p. 264.
8. *Ibid.*, pp. 266–67.
9. Mowrer, O. H. *The Crisis in Psychiatry and Religion*. Princeton, N.J.: D. Van Nostrand Company, Inc., 1961. p. 12.
10. Smith, J. E. *Reason and God*. New Haven, Conn.: Yale University Press, 1961, p. 261.

Chapter 1

1. Dawson, C. *The Dynamics of World History*. New York: New American Library, Inc., 1962, pp. 305–6.

2. Dostoevsky, F. *The Brothers Karamazov.* New York: Random House, Inc. (The Modern Library), 1950, pp. 289–90.
3. Durant, W. *Our Oriental Heritage.* New York: Simon and Schuster, 1954, p. 24.
4. ———. *The Lessons of History.* New York: Simon and Schuster, 1968, p. 81.
5. *Ibid.,* p. 18.
6. *Ibid.,* p. 46.
7. *Ibid.,* p. 20.
8. Hick, J. *Evil and the God of Love.* New York: Harper & Row, Publishers, Incorporated, 1966, pp. 369, 371.
9. Hume, D. *Dialogues Concerning Natural Religion.* New York: Hafner Publishing Company, Inc., 1969, part x, p. 66.
10. Huxley, J. *Religion without Revelation.* New York: Harper & Row, Publishers, Incorporated, 1957, p. 55.
11. James, W. *The Varieties of Religious Experience.* New York: Random House, Inc. (The Modern Library), 1929, p. 358.
12. *Ibid.,* p. 83.
13. *Ibid.,* p. 243.
14. Kaufmann, W. *The Faith of a Heretic.* Garden City, N.Y.: Doubleday & Company, Inc. (Anchor Books), 1963, p. 167.
15. Lovejoy, A. O. *The Great Chain of Being.* Cambridge, Mass.: Harvard University Press, 1950, p. 65.
16. Löwith, K. *Meaning in History.* Chicago: The University of Chicago Press, 1949, p. 3.
17. *Ibid.,* p. 25.
18. Maddi, S. A. "The Existential Neurosis." *Journal of Abnormal Psychology,* 1967, 72, No. 4, 311–35.
19. Manwell, R. D. "An Insect Pompeii." In Engel, L. (ed.) *New Worlds of Modern Science.* New York: Dell Publishing Co., Inc., 1956, p. 196.
20. Muller, H. *The Uses of the Past.* New York: Oxford University Press (Mentor Books), 1954, p. 391.
21. Nietzsche, F. *The Genealogy of Morals.* London: 1913, p. 103.
22. Robertson, J. G. *The Life and Work of Goethe.* New York: E. P. Dutton & Co., Inc., 1932, p. 321.
23. *Ibid.,* p. 322.
24. Schjelderup-Ebbe. Quoted in Allee, W. C. *The Social Life of Animals.* New York: W. W. Norton & Company, Inc., 1938, p. 185.
25. Simpson, G. G. *The Meaning of Evolution.* New Haven, Conn.: Yale University Press, 1967, pp. 193–94.

26. *Ibid.*, pp. 344–45.
27. Stace, W. T. *Religion and the Modern Mind.* New York: J. B. Lippincott Company, 1952, pp. 223–24.
28. *Ibid.*, p. 168.
29. ———— "Man against Darkness." In Weeks, E., and Flint, E. (eds.) *Jubilee: One Hundred Years of the Atlantic.* Boston: Little, Brown and Company, 1957, pp. 380, 383.
30. Tolstoy, L. N. *My Confession; My Religion: The Gospel in Brief.* New York: Thomas Y. Crowell Company, 1899, pp. 19–20.
31. Ward, L. Quoted in Durant, W. *Our Oriental Heritage.* New York: Simon and Schuster, 1954, p. 23.
32. Zweig, S. *Master Builders: A Typology of the Spirit.* New York: The Viking Press, Inc., 1939, pp. 827, 828, 829.

CHAPTER 2

1. Barbour, I. G. *Issues in Science and Religion.* Englewood Cliffs, N.J.: Prentice-Hall, Inc., 1966, p. 344.
2. Bertalanffy, L. von. *General System Theory.* New York: George Braziller, Inc., 1968, pp. 191–92.
3. *Ibid.*, pp. 152–53.
4. ————. *Problems of Life.* New York: John Wiley & Sons, Inc., 1952, p. 105.
5. Bigelow, R. *The Dawn Warriors.* Boston: Little, Brown and Company, 1966, p. 236.
6. Birch, L. C. *Nature and God.* Philadelphia: The Westminster Press, 1965, p. 44.
7. Born, M. *Natural Philosophy of Cause and Chance.* London: Oxford University Press, 1949.
8. Darwin, F. (ed.) *Life and Letters of Charles Darwin.* New York: D. Appleton and Company, Inc., 1887, vol. I, pp. 279–82.
9. *Ibid.*, p. 54.
10. Haldane, J. B. S. *The Causes of Evolution.* Ithaca, N.Y.: Cornell University Press, 1966, p. 162.
11. Hardy, A. *The Living Stream,* New York: Harper & Row, Publishers, Incorporated, 1965, p. 211.
12. *Ibid.*, p. 184.
13. *Ibid.*, p. 170.
14. *Ibid.*, p. 146.

15. *Ibid.*, p. 137.
16. *Ibid.*, p. 198.
17. Hartshorne, C. *Beyond Humanism.* Lincoln: University of Nebraska Press (Bison Books), 1969, p. 164.
18. Koestler, A. *The Ghost in the Machine.* New York: The Macmillan Company, 1967, p. 158.
19. Lorenz, K. *The Evolution and Modification of Behavior.* Chicago: The University of Chicago Press, 1965, p. 29.
20. Maslow, A. H. *Toward a Psychology of Becoming.* Princeton, N.J.: D. Van Nostrand Company, Inc., 1968, p. 161.
21. ———. *Religion, Values, and Peak Experiences.* Columbus, Ohio: Ohio State University Press, 1964, p. 19.
22. Peacocke, A. R. "The Molecular Organization of Life." In Ramsey, I. L. (ed.) *Biology and Personality.* Oxford: Basil Blackwell & Mott, Ltd., 1965, pp. 35–36.
23. Pfeiffer, J. E. *The Emergence of Man.* New York: Harper and Row, Publishers, Incorporated, 1969, p. 220.
24. Russell, B. *Mysticism and Logic.* New York: Doubleday & Company, Inc., 1957, p. 45.
25. Schweitzer, A. "Out of My Life and Thought." In Burnett, W. (ed.) *The World's Best.* New York: The Dial Press, Inc., 1950, p. 820.
26. Simpson, G. G. *The Meaning of Evolution.* New Haven, Conn.: Yale University Press, 1967, p. 293.
27. Sinnott, E. *The Biology of the Spirit.* New York: The Viking Press, Inc., 1957, p. 161.
28. *Ibid.*, pp. 35–36.
29. *Ibid.*, p. 106.
30. *Ibid.*, p. 64.
31. *Ibid.*, p. 102.
32. *Ibid.*, p. 61.
33. ———. *Matter, Mind and Man.* New York: Harper & Brothers, 1957, pp. 137–38.
34. Teilhard de Chardin, P. Quoted in Raven, C. E. *Teilhard de Chardin: Scientist and Seer.* New York: Harper & Row, Publishers, Incorporated, 1963, p. 135.
35. Waddington, C. H. *The Nature of Life.* New York Harper & Row, Publishers, Incorporated (Harper Torchbooks), 1966, p. 89.
36. Weidenreich, C. Quoted from *Apes, Giants and Men.* In Dobzhansky, T. *The Biological Basis of Human Freedom.* New York: Columbia University Press, 1956, p. 104.

37. Whitehead, A. N. *The Function of Reason*. Boston: Beacon Press, 1958, p. 7.
38. Zweig, S. *Master Builders: A Typology of the Spirit*. New York: The Viking Press, Inc., 1939, p. 243.

CHAPTER 3

1. Amiel, H. F. *The Private Journal of Henri F. Amiel*. New York: The Macmillan Company, 1935, p. 149.
2. Bertalanffy, L. von *General System Theory*. New York: George Braziller, Inc., 1968, p. 191.
3. *Ibid.*, p. 194.
4. Breasted, J. H. *The Dawn of Conscience*. New York: Charles Scribner's Sons, 1961, p. 410.
5. *Ibid.*, p. xxix.
6. *Ibid.*, p. xv.
7. *Ibid.*, p. xvi.
8. *Ibid.*, p. 498.
9. *Ibid.*, p. 513.
10. Dobzhansky, T. *The Biological Basis of Human Freedom*. New York: Columbia University Press, 1956, p. 126.
11. *Ibid.*, p. 125.
12. *Ibid.*, p. 129.
13. ————. *Mankind Evolving*. New York: Bantam Books, Inc., 1970, p. 351.
14. Einstein, A. Quoted in Bochner, S. "The Role of Mathematics in the Rise of Science." *Science*, 1971, 174, p. 617.
15. Huntington, E. *Mainsprings of Civilization*. New York: New American Library, Inc. (Mentor Books), 1959, p. 35.
16. Huxley, T. H. *Evolution and Ethics*. New York: D. Appleton & Company, Inc., 1896, p. 83.
17. Huxley, J. *Evolution in Action*. Harper & Brothers, 1953, p. 146.
18. Kropotkin, P. *Mutual Aid: A Factor in Evolution*. Boston: Extending Horizons Books, (n.d.), p. 300.
19. *Ibid.*, p. 58.
20. Montagu, A. *The Natural Superiority of Women*. New York: The Macmillan Company, 1968, p. 157.
21. *Ibid.*, p. 162.
22. Simpson, G. G. *The Meaning of Evolution*. New Haven, Conn.: Yale University Press, 1967, p. 316.

23. Sorokin, P. A. *The Ways and Power of Love*. Chicago: Henry Regnery Company (Gateway Editions), 1967, p. 128.
24. *Ibid.*, p. 65.
25. Tinbergen, N. *Social Behavior in Animals*. London: Chapman & Hall, Ltd., 1953, p. 21.

CHAPTER 4

1. Allport, G. *The Individual and His Religion*. New York: The Macmillan Company, 1959, p. 93.
2. Barraclough, G. "The Historian in a Changing World." In Meyerhoff, H. (ed.) *The Philosophy of History in our Time*. New York: Doubleday & Company, Inc. (Anchor Books), 1959, p. 30.
3. Berdyaev, N. *The Meaning of History*. New York: The World Publishing Company (Meridian Books), 1962, p. 163.
4. Bertalanffy, L. von *General System Theory*. New York: George Braziller, Inc., 1968, p. 204.
5. Bloch, I. *Marquis de Sade*. New York: Brittany Press (Castle Books), 1948, p. 70.
6. Burtt, E. A. *Types of Religious Philosophy*. New York: Harper & Row, Publishers, Incorporated, 1939, p. 37.
7. Bury, J. B. *The Idea of Progress*. New York: Dover Publications, Inc., 1955.
8. Carr, E. H. *The New Society*. Boston: Beacon Press, 1957, p. 5.
9. ———. *What is History*. New York: Random House, Inc. (Vintage Books), 1967, p. 187.
10. Cohen, M. R. *The Meaning of Human History*. La Salle, Ill.: The Open Court Publishing Company, 1947, p. 279.
11. *Ibid.*, p. 266.
12. Cousins, N. Editorial in *Saturday Review*, 11-20-71.
13. Dawson, C. *The Dynamics of World History*. New York: New American Library, Inc., 1962, p. 254.
14. *Ibid.*, p. 233.
15. *Ibid.*, p. 308.
16. *Ibid.*, p. 291.
17. *Ibid.*, pp. 246, 254, 266.
18. Dobzhansky, T. "Of Flies and Men." In *American Psychologist*, 1966.
19. ———. *The Biological Basis of Human Freedom*. New York: Columbia University Press, 1956, p. 78.

20. ———. *The Biology of Ultimate Concern*. New York: New American Library, Inc., 1967, p. 125.
21. Dray, W. H. *Philosophy of History*. New York: Prentice-Hall, Inc., 1964, p. 80.
22. Durant, W. *The Age of Faith*. New York: Simon and Schuster, 1950, p. 73.
23. ———. *The Lessons of History*. New York: Simon and Schuster, 1968, p. 98.
24. Harrington, M. *The Accidental Century*. Baltimore: Penguin Books, Inc., 1966, pp. 22, 23.
25. Hegel, G. W. F. *The Philosophy of Right; the Philosophy of History*. Chicago: Encyclopaedia Britannica, Inc. (Hutchins, R. W. [ed.]: *Great Books of the Western World*), 1952, vol. 46, p. 161.
26. Heilbroner, R. L. *The Worldly Philosophers*. New York: Simon and Schuster, 1953, p. 25.
27. Huntington, E. *Mainsprings of Civilization*. New York: New American Library, Inc. (Mentor Books), 1959, p. 25.
28. *Ibid.*, p. 61.
29. *Ibid.*
30. *Ibid.*, p. 167.
31. *Ibid.*, p. 168.
32. *Ibid.*, p. 217.
33. Huxley, T. H. and Huxley, J. *Touchstone for Ethics*. New York: Harper & Brothers, 1947, p. 200.
34. Huxley, J. *Evolution in Action*. New York: Harper & Brothers (Mentor Books), 1953, p. 146.
35. Kroeber, A. L. *Anthropology: Culture Patterns and Processes*. New York: Harcourt, Brace & World, Inc. (Harbinger Books), 1963, p. 93.
36. *Ibid.*, p. 193.
37. Lifton, R. J. "Beyond Atrocity." In *Saturday Review*, 3-27-71.
38. Löwith, K. *Meaning in History*. Chicago: The University of Chicago Press, 1949, p. 4.
39. *Ibid.*, p. 55.
40. *Ibid.*, p. 112.
41. *Ibid.*, p. 6.
42. *Ibid.*, p. 7.
43. Mazlish, B. *The Riddle of History*. New York: Harper & Row, Publishers, Incorporated, 1966, p. 10.
44. Maslow, A. H. *New Knowledge of Human Values*. Chicago: Henry Regnery Company (Gateway Editions), 1970, pp. 125–27.

45. Meyerhoff, H. *The Philosophy of History in Our Time*. Garden City, New York: Doubleday & Company, Inc., 1959, p. 21.
46. Moorehead, A. *The Russian Revolution*. New York: Harper & Brothers, 1958, p. 7.
47. *Ibid.*, p. 161.
48. Muller, H. J. *The Uses of the Past*. New York: New American Library, Inc., 1954, p. 79.
49. *Ibid.*, p. 393.
50. ———. *Freedom in the Western World*. New York: Harper & Row, Publishers, Incorporated (Colophon Books), 1964, p. 350.
51. *Ibid.*, p. 54.
52. *Ibid.*, p. 55.
53. *Ibid.*, p. 290.
54. *Ibid.*, p. xv.
55. *Ibid.*, p. xvi.
56. *Ibid.*, p. xix.
57. O'Neill, E. In *New York Tribune*. February 1921.
58. Spengler, O. *The Decline of the West*. New York: Alfred A. Knopf, Inc., 1947, vol. I, p. 3.
59. *Ibid.*, p. 39.
60. Tiger, L., and Fox, R. *The Imperial Animal*. New York: Holt, Rinehart and Winston, Inc., 1971, p. 233.
61. *Ibid.*, p. 206.
62. *Ibid.*, pp. 208, 210, 211.
63. Vico, G. *The New Science of Giambattista Vico*. Bergin, T. G., and Fisch, M. H. (eds.). New York: Doubleday & Company, Inc. (Anchor Books), 1961, p. 60.
64. *Ibid.*, p. 27.
65. Walsh, W. H. *Philosophy of History*. New York: Harper & Row, Publishers, Incorporated (Torch Books), 1967, p. 119.

CHAPTER 5

1. Barbour, I. G. *Issues in Science and Religion*. Englewood Cliffs, N.J.: Prentice-Hall, Inc., 1966, p. 131.
2. *Ibid.*, p. 53.
3. Berdyaev, N. *The Meaning of History*. New York: The World Publishing Company (Meridian Books), 1962.

4. *Ibid.*, pp. 57–58.
5. ———. *The Destiny of Man*. London: Geoffrey Bles, Ltd., 1948, p. 25.
6. *Ibid.*, p. 32.
7. *Ibid.*, p. 43.
8. Birch, L. C. *Nature and God*. Philadelphia: The Westminster Press, 1965, p. 103.
9. *Ibid.*, p. 45.
10. *Ibid.*, p. 100.
11. Blanshard, B. In Hook, S. (ed.) *Determinism and Freedom*. London: Collier-Macmillan, Ltd. (Collier Books), 1961, p. 24.
12. Boisen, A. *Religion in Crisis and Custom*. New York: Harper & Brothers, 1955, pp. 112–13, 118, 162.
13. Burtt, E. A. *Types of Religious Philosophy*. New York: Harper & Row, Publishers, Incorporated, 1939, p. 406.
14. *Ibid.*, p. 31.
15. Butterfield, H. *The Englishman and His History*. Cambridge University Press, 1944, p. 103.
16. Carr, E. H. *What Is History*. New York: Random House, Inc. (Vintage Books), 1967, p. 62.
17. Dewey, J. *A Common Faith*. New Haven, Conn.: Yale University Press, 1934, p. 35.
18. Dobzhansky, T. "Of Flies and Men." In *American Psychologist*, 1966, pp. 41–46.
19. Durant, W. and Durant, A. *The Lessons of History*. New York: Simon and Schuster, 1968, p. 46.
20. Durant, W. *Our Oriental Heritage*. New York: Simon and Schuster, 1954, p. 320.
21. Gide, A. *Journals*. New York: Alfred A. Knopf, Inc., 1956, vol. II, p. 292.
22. Hallowell, A. I. "Culture, Personality and Society." In Tax, S. (ed.) *Anthropology Today*. Chicago: The University of Chicago Press, 1962, pp. 366–67.
23. Hamilton, E. *The Greek Way*. New York: W. W. Norton and Company, Inc. (Norton Library), 1964, pp. 165, 167.
24. Hobart, R. E. In Berofsky, B. (ed.) *Free Will and Determinism*. New York: Harper & Row, Publishers, Incorporated, 1966, p. 70.
25. James, W. *Radical Empiricism; A Pluralistic Universe*. New York: Longmans, Green & Co., Ltd., 1943, p. 311.
26. ———. *The Varieties of Religious Experience*. New York: Random House, Inc. (The Modern Library), 1929, p. 371.

27. *Ibid.*, p. 415.
28. *Ibid.*, p. 379.
29. *Ibid.*, p. 469.
30. Kaufmann, W. *The Faith of a Heretic*. Garden City, N.Y.: Doubleday & Company, Inc. (Anchor Books), 1963, p. 137.
31. *Ibid.*, p. 139.
32. *Ibid.*, p. 186.
33. ———. *Critique of Religion and Philosophy*. Garden City, N.Y.: Doubleday & Company, Inc. (Anchor Books), 1961, p. 317.
34. *Ibid.*, p. 325.
35. *Ibid.*, pp. 328–330.
36. Mann, T. Quoted in Neider, C. *The Stature of Thomas Mann*. New York: James Laughlin, 1947, p. 229.
37. Maslow, A. H. "Religious Aspects of Peak-Experiences." In Sadler, W. A. *Personality and Religion*. New York: Harper and Row, Publishers, Incorporated, 1970, p. 178.
38. ———. *Toward a Psychology of Becoming*. Princeton, N.J.: D. Van Nostrand Company, Inc., 1968, p. 12.
39. May, R. *Psychology and the Human Dilemma*. Princeton, N.J.: D. Van Nostrand Company, Inc., 1967, p. 143.
40. McNeill, W. H. *The Rise of the West*. Chicago: The University of Chicago Press, 1963, p. 344.
41. McTaggart, J. *Some Dogmas of Religion*. In Kaufmann, W. (ed.) *Religion from Tolstoy to Camus*. New York: Harper & Row, Publishers, Incorporated (Torchbooks), 1964, p. 462.
42. Mill, J. S. Quoted in Berofsky, *op. cit.*, p. 170.
43. Nietzsche, F. *Ecce Homo*. New York: Russell & Russell, Inc., 1964, pp. 101–02.
44. Otto, R. *Mysticism: East and West*. New York: The Macmillan Company, 1932.
45. ———. *The Idea of the Holy*. London: Oxford University Press, 1958.
46. Pahnke, W. H. "Implications of LSD and Experimental Mysticism." In *Journal of Religion and Health*, 1966, 5 No. 3, 175–208.
47. *Ibid.*, p. 192.
48. Royce, J. Quoted in Kaufmann, W. *Religion from Tolstoy to Camus*. New York: Harper & Row, Publishers, Incorporated (Torchbooks), 1961, p. 247.
49. Schelling, F. W. J. *The Ages of the World*. New York: Columbia University Press, 1942, p. 225.

50. Smith, J. E. *Reason and God.* New Haven, Conn.: Yale University Press, 1961, pp. 256–57.
51. Spinoza, B. *The Chief Works of Benedict de Spinoza.* (Elwes, R. H. M., ed.) New York: Dover Publications, Inc., 1951, vol. II, pp. 75, 119, 135.
52. Stace, W. T. "Man against Darkness." In Weeks, E., and Flint, E. (eds.) *Jubilee: One Hundred Years of the Atlantic.* Boston: Little, Brown and Company, 1957, pp. 377–85.
53. ———. *The Teachings of the Mystics.* New York: New American Library, Inc. (Mentor Books), 1960, p. 236.
54. *Ibid.*, p. 16.
55. *Ibid.*, p. 239.
56. Thomas, G. F. *Religious Philosophies of the West.* New York: Charles Scribner's Sons, 1965, p. 140.
57. Weber, M. *From Max Weber: Essays in Sociology.* (Gerth, H. H., and Mills, C. W. [eds.] New York: Oxford University Press, 1972, p. 287.
58. Wieman, H. N. *The Source of Human Good.* Carbondale, Ill.: Southern Illinois University Press, 1946, pp. 96–97.
59. Whitehead, A. N. *Process and Reality.* New York: The Macmillan Company, 1957, p. 532.
60. *Ibid.*, p. 377.
61. *Ibid.*, p. 529.
62. *Ibid.*, p. 306.
63. *Ibid.*, p. 307.

Chapter 6

1. Adolfs, R. "Is God Dead?" In Murchland, B. *The Meaning of the Death of God.* New York: Vintage Books, 1967, p. 83.
2. Allport, G. *The Individual and His Religion.* New York: The Macmillan Company, 1959, p. 2.
3. *Ibid.*, pp. 10–11.
4. *Ibid.*, p. 38.
5. *Ibid.*, p. 26.
6. *Ibid.*, pp. 14–15.
7. *Ibid.*, p. 76.
8. *Ibid.*, p. 71.
9. *Ibid.*, p. 74.
10. *Ibid.*, p. 106.
11. Bakan, D. *Disease, Pain and Sacrifice.* Boston: Beacon Press, 1971, p. 47.

12. Barbour, I. G. *Issues in Science and Religion.* Englewood Cliffs, N.J.: Prentice-Hall, Inc., 1966, p. 215.
13. Boisen, A. *The Exploration of the Inner World.* New York: Harper & Brothers, 1944, p. 268.
14. ————. *Religion in Custom and Crisis.* New York: Harper & Brothers, 1955, p. xiii.
15. Bowra, C. M. *Classical Greece.* New York: Time, Inc., 1965, p. 51.
16. Bradford, L. P. In Bradford, L. P., Gibb, J. R., and Benne, K. D. *T-Group Theory and Laboratory Method.* New York: John Wiley & Sons, Inc., 1964, pp. 195–98.
17. Buber, M. *I and Thou.* Charles Scribner's Sons, 1958, p. 135.
18. ————. *Between Man and Man.* New York: The Macmillan Company, 1965.
19. Burtt, E. A. *Types of Religious Philosophy.* New York: Harper and Row, Publishers, Incorporated, 1939, p. 344.
20. *Ibid.,* p. 345.
21. Dewey, J. *A Common Faith.* New Haven, Conn.: Yale University Press, 1934, pp. 11–12.
22. *Ibid.,* p. 12.
23. *Ibid.,* p. 17.
24. Dostoevski, R. *The Brothers Karamazov.* New York: The Macmillan Company, 1955, pp. 314–15.
25. Dunne, J. S. "The Myth of God's Death." In Murchland, B. (ed.), *The Meaning of the Death of God.* New York: Vintage Books, 1967, p. 166.
26. Durant, W. *Our Oriental Heritage.* New York: Simon and Schuster, 1954, p. 640.
27. *Ibid.,* p. 784.
28. *Ibid.,* p. 787.
29. *Ibid.,* p. 795.
30. ————. *The Life of Greece.* New York: Simon and Schuster, 1939, p. 360.
31. *Ibid.,* p. 371.
32. Einstein, A. In Schlipp, P. A. (ed.) *Albert Einstein: Philosopher-Scientist.* New York: Harper & Row, Publishers, Incorporated (Harper Torchbooks), 1959, p. 5.
33. Gaer, J. *What the Great Religions Believe.* New York: Dodd, Mead & Company, Inc., 1963, p. 275.
34. *Ibid.,* pp. 96–97.
35. Grant, V. W. *The Psychology of Sexual Emotion.* New York: Longmans, Green & Co., Ltd., 1957, p. 13.

36. ———. *Great Abnormals.* New York: Hawthorne Books, Inc., 1968, pp. 73–126.
37. Hallie, P. In Shinn, R. L. (ed.) *Restless Adventure: Essays in Contemporary Expression of Existentialism.* New York: Charles Scribner's Sons, 1968, p. 30.
38. Hamilton, E. *The Greek Way.* New York: W. W. Norton & Company, Inc. (Norton Library), 1964, p. 174.
39. *Ibid.,* p. 25.
40. *Ibid.,* p. 186.
41. Huxley, J. *Religion without Revelation.* New York: Harper & Row, Publishers, Incorporated, 1957, pp. 55–56.
42. James, W. *The Varieties of Religious Experience.* New York: Random House, Inc. (The Modern Library), 1929, p. 28.
43. *Ibid.,* p. 430.
44. *Ibid.,* p. 485.
45. *Ibid.,* pp. 488–89.
46. *Ibid.,* p. 499.
47. *Ibid.,* p. 502.
48. Johnson, R. E. *Personality and Religion.* Nashville, Tenn.: Abingdon Press, 1957, p. 128.
49. *Ibid.,* p. 209.
50. *Ibid.,* p. 215.
51. *Ibid.,* pp. 219, 220, 223–24.
52. ———. *The Psychology of Religion.* Nashville, Tenn.: Abingdon Press, 1959, p. 182.
53. *Ibid.,* p. 183.
54. Kaufmann, W. *The Faith of a Heretic.* Garden City, N.Y.: Doubleday & Company, Inc. (Anchor Books), 1963, p. 372.
55. Lamont, C. *The Philosophy of Humanism.* New York: Frederick Ungar Publishing Company, 1965, pp. 285–89.
56. *Ibid.,* pp. 15, 16.
57. Lin Yutang. In Hellerman, L., and Stein, A. L. (eds.) *China: Readings in the Middle Kingdom.* New York: Washington Square Press, 1971, p. 86.
58. McNeill, W. H. *The Rise of the West.* Chicago: The University of Chicago Press, 1963, p. 323.
59. Miller, W. *Russians as People.* New York: E. P. Dutton & Co., Inc., 1961, pp. 78, 85, 89.
60. Mowrer, O. H. *The Crisis in Religion and Psychiatry.* Princeton, N.J.: D. Van Nostrand Company, Inc., 1961, p. 12.
61. ———. *The New Group Therapy.* Princeton, N.J.: D. Van Nostrand Company, Inc., 1964, p. x.

62. *Ibid.*, p. 24.
63. *Ibid.*, p. 19.
64. Muller, H. J. *The Uses of the Past.* New York: New American Library, Inc. (Mentor Books), 1952, p. 387.
65. *Ibid.*, pp. 357–58.
66. *Ibid.*, p. 363.
67. *Ibid.*, p. 368.
68. *Ibid.*, p. 391.
69. *Ibid.*, p. 152.
70. *Ibid.*, p. 155.
71. Nietzsche, F. Quoted from "Schopenhauer as Educator" in Kaufmann, W. *Existentialism from Dostoevski to Camus.* New York: The World Publishing Company (Meridian Books), 1956, pp. 101–2.
72. O'Dea, T. F. In Sadler, W. A. (ed.) *Personality and Religion.* New York: Harper & Row, Publishers, Incorporated, 1970, pp. 187–88.
73. Randall, J. H., Jr. *The Meaning of Religion for Man.* New York: Harper & Row, Publishers, Incorporated (Harper Torchbooks), 1968, pp. 56–57.
74. Rogers, C. R. "Some Directions and End Points in Therapy." In Mowrer, O. H. (ed.) *Psycho-therapy: Theory and Research.* New York: The Ronald Press Company, 1953, p. 50.
75. Russell, B. *The Conquest of Happiness.* New York: Liveright Publishing Company, 1930, p. 230.
76. Sadler, W. A. "The Scientific Study of Religion and Personality." In Sadler, W. A. (ed.) *Personality and Religion.* New York: Harper & Row, Publishers, Incorporated, 1970, pp. 3–4.
77. Santayana, G. *Reason in Society. (The Life of Reason,* vol. II), New York: Charles Scribner's Sons, 1936, p. 22.
78. Schoen, M. *Thinking about Religion.* New York: Philosophical Library, Inc., 1946, p. 42.
79. Sorokin, P. A. *The Ways and Power of Love.* Chicago: Henry Regnery Company (Gateway Editions), 1967, p. 61.
80. Thomas, H. F. In Burton, A. (ed.) *Encounter: Theory and Practice of Encounter Groups.* San Francisco: Jossey-Bass, Inc., 1970, p. 75.
81. *Time Magazine.* "The Mind of China." Time, Inc., vol. 89, 3-17-67.
82. Titus, H. H. *Living Issues in Philosophy.* New York: American Book Company, 1964, pp. 215–21.
83. Toffler, A. *Future Shock.* New York: Random House, Inc., 1970, p. 88.

84. *Ibid.*, p. 292.
85. Tolstoy, L. N. *Anna Karenina*. New York: New American Library, Inc., 1961, p. 118.
86. Tournier, P. *The Meaning of Persons*. New York: Harper & Brothers, 1957, pp. 179–97.
87. Vico, G. *The New Science of Giambattista Vico*. New York: Doubleday & Company, Inc. (Anchor Books), 1961.
88. Yalom, I. D. *The Theory and Practice of Group Psychotherapy*. New York: Basic Books, Inc., Publishers, 1970, p. 351.
89. *Ibid.*, pp. 351–52.
90. Yankelovich, D. "The New Naturalism: A Study of the Sources." *Saturday Review*, 4-1-72.
91. *Ibid.*